The Occult Connection

THE
Unexplained

The Occult Connection

The ways in which man has tried to make sense of his universe

Editor: Peter Brookesmith

BLACK CAT

Acknowledgments
Photographs were supplied by Aldus Archive, Associated
Newspapers, Associated Press, BBC Hulton Picture Library,
BBC Radio Times, Biblioteca Estensa Modena, Bibliothèque
Nationale Paris, Bilderdienst Suddeutsches, Janet and Colin
Bord, Bridgeman Art Library, Michael Brierley, British
Library, British Museum, Jean-Loup Charmet, Chronicle
Publishing Company, Peter Clayton, Aleister Crowley,
Daily Telegraph Colour Library, J.M. Dent and Sons Ltd,
Arnold Desser, Euston Films, Robert Estall, Mary Evans
Picture Library, Professor Eysenck, Werner Forman
Archive, Fortean Picture Library, Charles Walker Library,
Gulbenkian Museum/Durham, Sonia Halliday, Hamlyn
Group, Michael Holford, Ellich Howe, Robert Hunt
Library, Imperial War Museum, Kobal Collection,
Kuntshistorisches Museum/Vienna, Mansell Collection,
Metropolitan Museum of Art/New York, Museum of Fine
Arts/Antwerp, William MacQuitty, Naprstek Museum/
Prague, National Museum of Anthropology/Mexico, The
Photographers' Collection, Photoresources, Popperfoto,
Press Association, Harry Price Library, Rex Features, Scala,
Ronald Sheridan, Spectrum Colour Library, Suddeutscher
Verlag, Wiener Library, UKAEA, USIS, ZEFA.

Consultants to
The Unexplained
Professor A.J. Ellinson
Dr J. Allen Hynek
Brian Inglis
Colin Wilson
Editorial Director
Brian Innes
Editor
Peter Brookesmith
Deputy Editor
Lynn Picknett
Executive Editor
Lesley Riley
Sub Editors
Mitzi Bales
Chris Cooper
Jenny Dawson
Hildi Hawkins

Picture Researchers
Anne Horton
Paul Snelgrove
Frances Vargo
Editorial Manager
Clare Byatt
Art Editor
Stephen Westcott
Designer
Richard Burgess
Art Buyer
Jean Morley
Production Co-ordinator
Nicky Bowden
Volume Editors
Lorrie Mack
Francis Ritter

Material in this publication previously
appeared in the weekly partwork
The Unexplained, © 1980-83

This edition copyright © 1984 Orbis Publishing Ltd
copyright © 1988 Macdonald & Co (Publishers) Ltd

First published 1984 by Orbis Publishing Ltd
Reprinted 1988 by Macdonald & Co (Publishers) Ltd under
the Black Cat imprint

Macdonald & Co (Publishers) Ltd
3rd Floor, Greater London House
Hampstead Road, London NW1 7QX

a member of Maxwell Pergamon Publishing Corporation plc

ISBN 0-7481-0144-6

Printed in Belgium

Contents

Introduction

FACED WITH PESTILENCE, hunger, debt, grief, corruption, banditry, fire, flood and all the misfortune and misery that fate can bestow on humanity, people everywhere and in all ages have tried to discover a secret consistency underlying the inconstancy of existence. Most societies are cemented, at least in part, by the fact that they agree largely on the clues that may lead to the revelation of this redeeming, stable ground of being. In the West, we have subscribed for nearly 2000 years to the ethics and metaphysics of Christianity. But there have always been individuals who the generally accepted ideas have failed to console or satisfy: dissidents, intellectual buccaneers and adventurers — heretics or madmen to many of their contemporaries. A few of these souls (depraved as they must often have seemed) managed to convince some of their peers that there was wisdom in their quaint ideas; and, in time, those who inherited their beliefs saw them displace the prevailing wisdom and become the new form of orthodoxy. This was the story of the early Church: first persecuted without mercy by the Roman empire, it was at last proclaimed the official religion.

Yet there are some traditions that have never achieved this kind of ascendancy over the dominant beliefs of any age or society. They have existed for hundreds — in some cases for thousands — of years like a sort of intellectual and emotional undergrowth by the highway of conventional thought. They have been neither wholly tolerated nor entirely damned by the priesthood or the body politic. Astrology, once it had broken loose from its origins as the scientific forerunner of astronomy, became a system of arcane belief that attempted to give some order to our inscrutable destiny, and it has managed to survive with little enough harassment in widely different societies for centuries. Likewise, it seems reasonable to predict that another belief, that humanity will soon be relieved of responsibility for its own affairs by the advent of benign Space Beings (who are already watching over us), will probably persist in one form or another as long as we continue to probe the stars with elaborate forms of hardware.

But if these beliefs or systems of thought are so tenacious, why have they not dislodged the great religions, which are still so powerful in the affairs of men?

One part of the answer, I would suggest, is that they are not really in competition with the world's religions. It is true that both the religious outlook and the occult have in common a desire to decipher a meaning from the multifarious and confusing ways of the world. But each does so in its own distinct fashion, confronting different, if not entirely separate, mysteries. A religion tends to console its adherents, to counsel resignation to the outrages of fortune, and to provide a moral code whose observance, despite the manifest injustices of this life, will be rewarded hereafter. To that extent, a sense of religion is a sense of ultimate things; it is wrestling with the problem of life's meaning in the face of inevitable death. The occult systems, on the other hand, while also attempting to discern order amid the chaos (and in some cases suggesting that there are moral bases to their insights) are at once the more difficult and the more self-centred paths to 'enlightenment'. What has given the occult systems their extraordinary longevity is, as much as anything, their implicit claim to provide *the power to beat the system*. They offer not simply a means to withstand the pressures and problems of the world, but a way of getting out from under. One can control one's own fate, by foreseeing the future, by acquiring riches beyond the dreams of avarice, by entering the exclusive ranks of those chosen for salvation, by using occult 'powers' to achieve political mastery. Where religion is essentially passive, fatalistic and communal, the occult is active, individualistic, and self-serving.

One of the greatest explorations of this distinction between religion and the occult is the legend of Dr Faustus, most especially in the tragic treatment given it by Christopher Marlowe. Faustus allows his relentless curiosity and his desire for power to overcome him, and he loses his soul to the Devil, having gained a world that proves illusory. Faustus may have travelled in time, gained riches, fame, and the company of beautiful women, but he cannot in the end defy death. And therein may lie the one single reason why the occult has co-existed for so long with religion without really displacing it: for the occult offers no answer, finally, with which to deflect the attentions of the Great Reaper.

There is not, of course, any shortage of voices insisting that religion has no answers either, but is merely a distraction designed to keep the masses where they belong – oppressed, powerless, and afraid. A less ideological objection is that the consolations of religion are not based on demonstrable fact but on faith – a kind of cosmic wager that life's trials will all have been worthwhile. This is fair enough as far as it goes, but much the same argument can be raised against occult systems. It should, however, be easier for us to discover whether or not they work.

Certainly incautious predictions made by the UFO cults, such as the arrival of aid from the stars and the end of the world, have been embarrassingly inaccurate. Hitler's devotion to the musings of his astrologers did not prevent the onslaught of the Allied armies. No one has succeeded in transmuting lead into gold, not least because the instructions for doing so left by the alchemists of old are almost impenetrably obscure – they may even have been describing a spiritual rather than a material process.

At the same time it is fascinating to discover the astrological characteristics of one's best friends. As a Pisces with Sagittarius rising, I wonder if it is merely chance that the majority of my closest friends are Sagittarians? And are my capacities as a writer and editor somehow the result of being born under that most literary of signs, Pisces? Or what about the time I impertinently asked the same question of the *I Ching* three times, and it instructed me to be less frivolous, since I had asked the question twice before? The trouble is that most of the 'evidence' concerning divination systems is of this kind – anecdotal, impressionistic and unsatisfactory, because it lacks all statistical validity. And we all know people who have lost their sense of proportion when it comes to such systems, who can scarcely bring themselves to speak to anyone born under their opposing sign, or who cannot face the day if they do not first check it out with the *I Ching*. None of this improves the reputation of the system itself, even though such behaviour is scarcely the system's fault. In the following pages, at least, you will find a balanced assessment of the 'occult' – its origins, its significance and what it can (and cannot) do.

PETER BROOKESMITH

Saviours from the stars

Will the answers to humanity's problems come from the skies? Thousands of devoted believers in UFOs think they will. KEVIN McCLURE examines the 'flying saucer' cults and the contactees who are their prophets

OPINIONS ON THE true nature of UFOs vary widely, from the theory that they are as yet unexplained natural phenomena to the belief that they are illusions conjured up by demons to seduce mankind away from Christianity. If we bear in mind that such varying conclusions are all said to have been drawn from the same evidence and that such evidence is notoriously unreliable, then it appears that evidence and reason play a less important role in UFO belief than faith.

When faced with the unknown, the frightening, or the inexplicable, mankind tends to try to make it into a part of his religion: worships it, or damns it. UFO experience is no exception. Erich von Däniken believes that our religious history is actually one of UFO visitation and its misinterpretation. Arthur Shuttlewood, the chronicler of the mysterious events at Warminster in the southern

Members of the Aetherius Society charge a 'prayer battery' with spiritual energy on Wimbledon Common in London. They believe that the energy, when released under the direction of the Interplanetary Parliament, can assist troubled parts of the globe to struggle against spiritual danger

county of Wiltshire, England believes that UFOs are 'the giants of past ages in modern guise, ever reminding us that mankind faces many challenges before he completes his final life-cycle at the very hub of our wonder-filled universe'. Lord Clancarty, who writes under the name Brinsley le Poer Trench, believes in the 'Sky People', who left Earth after the sinking of Atlantis, and who are occupied now in helping us raise ourselves to a better state of life in the next millennium. There may well be a common source and stimulus for reported UFO, spiritist, ghostly and religious events, and this source is likely to be identified one day, with a resulting dramatic effect upon the world's beliefs and religious philosophies. But one can no more prove that one is right in these suspicions than can von Däniken, Shuttlewood or Trench. It is all assumption, guesswork, and a certain amount of faith or wishful thinking.

This type of belief about UFOs, while not capable of proof, seems justifiable and necessary; without it there would be little experimentation, few advances in understanding. So long as the believers remain

flexible and open-minded, there is no harm to come of it. But there is another form of UFO belief for which there is much less to be said, where reason seems to be wholly suspended, and where detailed and inflexible beliefs about UFOs – their origin, nature, occupants, and purpose – become an overwhelming form of religious faith or personal philosophy and outlook. The belief itself becomes a preoccupation, and a justification for all sorts of actions.

Such beliefs take a variety of forms. Some groups see ufonauts as seeking to co-operate with certain chosen individuals on the Earth, for the improvement or continuation of the quality of our life here. According to the teachings of such groups, the UFO people do not wish or promise to take their followers away. Two American 'contactee cults' are quite typical of many others.

The One World Family, founded by Allen-Michael Noonan, is a California-based cult that has attracted some following. Many of its features recur in numerous other groups. In Noonan's case, it is said that he was working on a billboard when he was suddenly transported to another planet. He found himself surrounded by angelic creatures, seated around a fluorescent throne. A voice boomed: 'Will you agree to be the Saviour of the world?' Noonan agreed. He has since remained in contact with an extra-terrestrial known as Ashtar, has made trips to an inhabited Venus, and regards himself as the Messiah. He is writing a massive reinterpretation of the Bible, the 'Everlasting Gospel', which his followers help him produce. He believes that he is the only mouthpiece for communications from Ashtar. Hallucinogenic drugs and the exercise of psychic abilities feature in the cult.

A new Messiah
Noonan also claims that, with the practical help of the aliens, the One World Family will eventually take over the government of the USA and the running of the United Nations; but only after all professing Christians have been, as they ambiguously phrase it, 'eliminated'. Allen-Michael Noonan is one of the least wholesome characters to have founded a UFO cult and it is impossible to tell whether or not he believes his own claims. But there is no doubt that his followers believe in both the claims and the individual, and try to act accordingly.

A less sinister, but none the less remarkable, cult group was the Institute for Cosmic Research, founded in Michigan, USA, in 1967 by a young man known as 'Gordon'. This group was developed around the supposed construction of a flying saucer that would actually fly – the *Bluebird* – and the group lasted as long as its members had faith in the unique achievement that would climax its slow and painstaking creation. Gordon claimed that his birth was supernatural: he arrived in his mother's arms, clad

Above: this flying disc was filmed by Daniel W. Fry (right) in Oregon, USA, in 1954. As a result of his many alleged contacts with space people, Fry works to enlighten mankind through an organisation called Understanding, Inc.

Above right: one of the earliest contactees, George Adamski, met a Venusian in 1952 and was subsequently instructed in the Cosmic Philosophy

in white muslin, while a UFO hovered over the house. He was, he said, one of the seven Great White Brothers (a common type of claim in pseudo-Eastern movements). He also affirmed that he, and he alone, was in contact with extra-terrestrial entities from Io, one of the moons of Jupiter. There, he said, he had represented Earth at meetings of the 'Intergalactic Council'.

He told his followers that the Space Brothers had warned him that 'Earth's vortex is about to break because of an excess amount of hatred on this planet.' However, the Space Brothers had a plan: in order to change the ways of mankind they had chosen 'to provide Gordon with the technology to build a small flying saucer.' Potential members of the institute were told that only highly developed souls could be involved in work on it. They were to build the saucer and fly it into the skies. They would be joined by saucers from other planets and together would circle Earth for three days, darkening the sky. People would look up and wonder

why – and then would fall on their knees and start practising 'universal law'.

In Gordon's cosmology, the Sun was cold, and the stars, all of them, were inhabited planets. Despite all this, which surely must have been hard to believe, it is clear that Gordon had considerable charisma. The group lasted seven years before the basic untruth of the claims dawned on his adherents. Even then, many of the group members were unwilling to accept the fact. It is desperately hard to admit that you have been *so* wrong, for *so* long. The group had expended time, money, energy and faith: in some ways it was easier to go on believing than to have to cope with reality.

The great majority of UFO contactee cults come from the USA and British ufology is largely free of such extreme beliefs. But the most famous and long-lived contactee cult of all was started in Britain in about 1955. The Aetherius Society, which now has its headquarters in the London suburb of Fulham, has established itself in several of the world's major cities and has members in over 40 countries. Hundreds of devoted members attend the society's activities in Britain and the USA.

The story of the Aetherius Society and its development is very much that of its founder, George King. He built the society from nothing and now is held in the highest esteem by its members. It is worth considering, in a field where cults and belief groups are mostly transient and ephemeral, why the Aetherius Society has achieved a relatively wide appeal and has lasted so long. The key elements of the society's doctrine are very similar to those of the One World Family and the Institute for Cosmic Research. It offered its adherents a cosmology that was then beyond scientific disproof. (It asserted that most of the solar system was inhabited.) It provided an explanation for a mystery that held a widespread fascination: the flying saucers being seen all over the world. Many of them, it was said, represented a benign and concerned force – the Interplanetary Parliament. The doctrine imposed a task on the society's members: to store up, in conjunction with the extra-terrestrial entities, 'spiritual energy' in 'spiritual batteries'

Above left: Allen Noonan, founder of the One World Family, based in California. He receives communications from an extra-terrestrial called Ashtar and regards himself as the Messiah

Left: Frank E. Stranges, president of International Evangelism Crusades, Inc., received guidance from a Venusian called Val Thor, who had come to 'help mankind return to the Lord'

Far left: a well-known New York broadcaster, Long John Nebel (holding photographs), with George W. van Tassel, who founded the Ministry of Universal Wisdom to pass on teachings gleaned from regular UFO contacts

metaphysical studies, even though we believed that we were on the verge of discovering a new method of cancer treatment which could cure certain forms of this malignant scourge. Nevertheless, this command came out of the blue in such a way that no receiver could do anything else but listen and obey . . . . Quite soon after the deliverance of the Command, I was able to tune in and receive, telepathically, information which was relayed over millions of miles of etheric space. A message from Venus was recorded on our tape recorder. . . .

To be a little sceptical, it might have been better for the world if George King had persisted with his work on cancer, for much of the information he said he had received and the experiences he claimed to have had, implausible enough at the time, have since been rendered utterly absurd by the discoveries of space exploration. King wrote of his travels to Venus and Mars, and stated that Mercury was the only uninhabited planet. He detailed a battle he fought on a massive flying saucer of an interplanetary space fleet, 40 million miles (64 million kilometres) from Earth. In public meetings he gave trance messages from entities such as Mars Sector 6, the Master Aetherius and even the Master Jesus, who was apparently living on or near Venus. Without this last claim, the society might have been taken a little more seriously.

However, in spite of the utter lack of verifiable evidence for any of King's claims,

located in high places all over the world. This energy could then be discharged to prevent hardship, disease and disaster around the world. Lastly, the society possessed a priest: a go-between or communicator who alone had the ear of the Interplanetary Parliament, who would pass on the messages of the extra-terrestrials, and in turn would represent his followers to the mightier powers beyond. That communicator was, of course, George King.

The roots of the Aetherius Society lie in King's fascination, prior to 1954, with yoga and Eastern philosophy and metaphysics. His early life is not well-known, but he was born in Shropshire in 1919 and at various times worked as a fire service employee and a hire-car driver, and ran a healing sanctuary.

The publicity material has it that one day in May 1954, when King was alone in his flat in west London, he heard a voice say: 'Prepare yourself! You are to become the voice of Interplanetary Parliament.' Eight days later 'an Indian Swami of world renown [who] had obviously walked straight through' the locked door gave him information and instruction that dramatically changed his life and led to the founding of the society. In *You are responsible* King, not known for his humility, explains that he had to forsake his

Above: Jupiter's innermost moon, Io. According to one 'Gordon', who founded the Institute for Cosmic Research in 1967, this world, slightly larger than our Moon, was the meeting place of the Intergalactic Council. If so, they chose a singularly inhospitable place. Space probes have discovered a world in violent turmoil, coloured reddish by sulphur spewed out by volcanoes larger than any on Earth

Right: publicity material of an Italian UFO contactee group, with a photograph allegedly showing their extra-terrestrial master. In 1976 this group wrote to US President Jimmy Carter, whose UFO sighting of a few years earlier had been widely reported. They told him that the authority he enjoyed had been 'granted from above'

The Venusian Candidate

Study Center of Cosmic Fraternity
DELEGATION OF THE U.S.A.
P. O. BOX 5 · 95028 VALVERDE (CT) ITALY

REAL PHOTOGRAPH OF
ADONIESIS

FROM THE HEAVENS TO EARTH

I am not of this world: Listen to me !

Non sono di questo mondo: Ascoltatemi !

Je ne suis pas de ce monde: Ecoutez-moi !

No soy de este mundo: Escuchadme !

Ich bin nicht von dieser Welt: Hoeret auf mich !

his meetings grew larger. A regular journal, the *Cosmic Voice*, was launched soon after the society's inception. The messages relayed by King in an apparent trance state were taken seriously and acted upon though, like this example from Mars Sector 6, they were not always very clear: 'Take those M-ions inside of yourself, then your brain cells will release an opposite female magnetic energy. This will counteract the hurricane-force.'

That the society still thrives may seem surprising, but members, who seem often to be selfless and determined, concentrate much of their efforts on the 'task' previously mentioned. They have made pilgrimages, often in difficult and dangerous conditions,

Below: George W. van Tassel, himself in regular contact with space beings, played host to UFO enthusiasts and other contactees at his Giant Rock Space Conventions, where participants watched for signals from UFOs – and sometimes saw them

Bottom: Mount Kilimanjaro, in East Africa, is a site of 'prayer energy' – thanks to the efforts of the Aetherius Society

picked up by Adepts 002 and 003 [extra-terrestrials] in position in their (invisible) Space Craft above the central base of operations in Los Angeles.' George King reported during the operation that 'the Great White Brotherhood Retreat in Kilimanjaro, East Africa, had now joined in the release pattern.' At the end of the operation, Mars Sector 6 informed King that 'there was a heavy resonance of Spiritual Energies over the whole of Poland.' Perhaps the society is mistaken in trying to explain the mechanics of how prayer works. Older, possibly wiser, faiths keep the whole matter as vague and obscure as they can.

Though good will and a sense of common purpose hold the Aetherius Society together, one feature seems sure to limit severely the number of those who take it seriously. From being plain George King in 1954, the leader of the Aetherius Society had by the end of 1981 become the holder of such titles as Knight Commander, Doctor of Philosophy, Doctor of Divinity, Doctor of Sacred Humanities, Metropolitan Archbishop of the Aetherius Churches and Count de Florina. Some of these titles are conferred by the Aetherius Society, others are awarded by what are said to be ancient chivalric orders. Similarly, the society is deep in Knights, Ladies, Reverends and Doctors. Even this, the most respectable of the UFO cults, seems unable to understand what impression such excesses make on outsiders.

to a number of the world's mountains to fulfil the aims of plans bearing such names as Operation Sunbeam, Operation Bluewater and Operation Starlight. They have charged the spiritual energy batteries in such places as Ben Macdhui in Scotland, Mount Kilimanjaro in Tanzania and the Madrigerfluh in Switzerland. On the night of 27 June 1981, for instance, batteries E-1 and E-3 were charged at Holdstone Down, in south-west England. The 160 members of the society who were present stored a total of 219 hours and 28 minutes of prayer energy in battery E-1. Meanwhile, the extra-terrestrials put 1100 hours into battery E-3. On the same weekend, as part of Operation Sunbeam, 6000 prayer hours of energy were sent from Jupiter to the Psychic Centre in Scotland.

It is easy to make fun of such behaviour. But if there is any element of truth in what the society believes, then its members deserve credit for their selfless efforts. In a recent *Cosmic Voice* it was reported that a discharge under Operation Prayer Power was sent to Poland on 23 April 1981. It was intended to help prevent a Russian invasion.

The mechanics of the discharge were complex. The Los Angeles battery had to be substituted for the inadequate Detroit one because: 'the Prayer Energies were not being

Apocalypse now?

Messianic UFO contactees often give detailed warnings of impending disasters. But the cults invariably insist that only their own chosen few will be saved – a promise that attracts hopeful devotees

MOST UFO CULTS have appeared in the United States, long the home of countless eccentric religious and near-religious groups. The story of one of these cults is told in full by a trio of sociologists, Leon Festinger, Henry Riecken and Stanley Schachter. They 'planted' observers in a developing group centred on a UFO 'communicator' in 'Lake City', Utah. (The authors used fictitious names throughout, in order to protect their subjects.) The communicator was 'Marian Keech', who believed she had received the initial message from her late father. She sat quietly and regularly thereafter, waiting to produce automatic writing. She was soon contacted by 'higher forces': first by 'the Elder Brother', and then by entities from the planets Clarion and Cerus (neither of which is known to conventional astronomy). She received communications especially from one Sananda of Clarion, who claimed to have been Jesus in an earlier time.

Mrs Keech did not publicise her messages enthusiastically, but others from existing UFO groups and mystical or occult groups soon showed an interest, and in August 1954 a press release was issued. This summarised

not only the more philosophical part of the communications, in which the media took little interest, but also predictions regarding a coming physical disaster of vast proportions. The nature of the event, as reported by Mrs Keech, varied at times, but as interest in the group grew its details became more firmly fixed. At the end of September the *Lake City Herald* published this typical report:

Lake City will be destroyed by a flood from Great Lake just before dawn, December 21st, according to a suburban housewife. Mrs Marian Keech of 847 West School Street says the prophecy is not her own. It is the purport of many messages she has received by automatic writing, she says . . . . The messages, according to Mrs Keech, are sent to her by superior beings from a planet called 'Clarion'. These beings have been visiting the Earth, she says, in what we call 'Flying Saucers'. During their visits, she says, they have observed fault lines in the Earth's crust that foretoken the deluge. Mrs Keech reports she was told the flood will spread to form an inland sea stretching from the Arctic Circle to the Gulf of Mexico.

By now Marian Keech was referring to a group of communicators whom she called the 'Guardians', though Sananda remained the most important. Once the media had

Left: in a television science fiction play a throng of young people, controlled by armed police, gather at an ancient stone circle in the expectation that UFOs are about to take them to a new existence beyond the Earth. Invocations of 'space people' have taken place at pop festivals and UFO enthusiasts' gatherings – where badges such as these (inset) find a ready market. Many older and rather more staid people, however, have also expected to be contacted by UFOs and delivered from imminent cataclysm

started to publicise the group, Mrs Keech and her associates began to be afflicted by the problems that always beset UFO contactees. Increasing numbers of visitors called at her house, often when group members were present. She had explained to the group that if they did the right thing and were gathered together, ready, at the appointed time, they would not be drowned in the forthcoming flood but would be carried away in one or more flying saucers. The extra-terrestrials could come to make contact at any time and in any way: so Mrs Keech and her group had to decide whether or not visitors were extra-terrestrials and also whether they were good or evil extra-terrestrials.

The last days

The cult had now fallen into the classical pattern: it had a communicator, an explanation for the UFO mystery, a message of great importance, and a 'task' for its members – not so much to publicise the disaster as to prepare themselves to survive it. As the chosen date approached, the visitors became more frequent and more outlandish. Members of the group gave up jobs, possessions and relationships, and some took up unusual diets. All who could came together to await the fulfilment of their expectations. One condition of escape required by the Guardians was that all metal should be removed from the participants' persons. This led to some interesting arrangements for trousers and brassières, and a lively discussion about dental fillings.

The last few days before 21 December were traumatic for the group members, as their hopes were first raised and then dashed by increasingly strange messages and predictions, all proving to be inaccurate. The

Above: salvation from ageing and death was promised by George van Tassel, the 'Sage of Giant Rock'. On instructions from extra-terrestrials he built this structure, the 'Integratron', at Giant Rock Airport in California, USA. It was intended for research into 'the unseen truths of life', and to develop techniques of preventing and even reversing the processes of ageing in the human body. The structure, four storeys high, was made mostly of timber, and contained no metal

greatest shock came on the day itself, when no flood arrived, nor any spacecraft to save them from it. The group fell prey to disillusion and in due course dispersed.

Another group that purveyed warnings of catastrophe transmitted from space beings called itself the 'Light Affiliates'. They were active in the late 1960s in Burnaby, British Columbia. Their launching statement read:

We wish to notify all those interested that a phenomenon has occurred here in Vancouver. A young girl, age 22, suddenly began channeling on 23.10.69. Her source is a being identifying himself as Ox-Ho, who is relaying transmissions from a galaxy close to our own . . . . Her material is phenomenal in that she has been informed of the coming disasters, when to expect them, and what to do pertaining to the necessary evacuation of the danger areas and food supplies, etc, that will be needed.

The real name of the 'channel' was Robin McPherson, but she was renamed 'Estelle' by the 'being'. Her mother Aileen became 'Magdalene', her friend Sally became 'Celeste'. A young man involved in the early communications was given the evocative name 'Truman Merit'.

Ox-Ho explained that the day of judgement would begin during 22 November 1969. In these final hours Man would be 'given a last opportunity to repair his decadent house before the terminal series of disasters'. If mankind did not take the opportunity to change, 'the Space Brothers would remove the Chosen and return them to Earth after the planet had once again "crystallised", and been spiritually, as well as physically, restructured.' The 'restructuring' would involve the tilting of the Earth on its

axis and the disappearance beneath the sea of large land areas. The members of the Light Affiliates were exhorted to evangelise wherever possible.

Nothing seems to have happened on the predicted date to fulfil the expectations of the Light Affiliates. Robin McPherson ceased to communicate, but her mother continued the task. In an interview with the writer Brad Steiger in the mid 1970s, she explained where the predictions had gone wrong:

We misinterpreted them, Brad, because it all happened so suddenly. The first visions I was given of destruction were very upsetting. I can see things now in a much broader perspective . . . . The thing is that it is the first ascension, and it is a *mental* ascension. The Brothers are trying to get as many people as possible into the Kingdom . . . . You know, I've been told by the Brotherhood that Earth is like an encounter therapy centre for the psychotics of the Universe . . . . I have been shown that the Earth is also wobbling very drastically on its axis.

It is sometimes less painful to find ways of showing that your beliefs are fundamentally correct by means of some elaborate reinterpretation than to concede that they are simply mistaken.

Claims that intelligent beings can visit us from the planets of the solar system have been made implausible by space exploration. Alien entities must come from distant star systems, even from other galaxies, of which science presently knows little. Some UFO cults – though by no means all – have adapted to the growth of knowledge by placing the source of their communications in suitably remote places.

The group that made the greatest impact

Above: Joan Culpepper tells reporters about her life with Human Individual Metamorphosis (HIM), the UFO cult run by the Two (below right). HIM offered its followers the prospect of being transported physically to a realm beyond the Earth's atmosphere. Joan Culpepper left the cult and set up a 'half-way house' to assist other disillusioned former adherents. Her two companions in this picture – still believing members of the cult – had taken the names 'Levi' and 'Moriah'. The Two called themselves Bo and Peep – but at the time the photograph was taken they bore their original names: Marshall Huff Applewhite and Bonnie Lu Trusdale Nettles. At the time they were under arrest by Texas police on charges of car theft and credit card fraud

during the 1970s was called HIM – Human Individual Metamorphosis. This group appeared in California in 1975 and appealed to some of those who had dabbled in the drug culture, personal spiritual development and 'New Age' mysticism. The movement was run by a middle-aged man and woman. They adopted names that were modest enough: Bo and Peep. Their teaching offered the advantages of life after death without the inconvenience of dying. Instead the adherents were to ascend physically. One of the cult's publicity posters read:

UFOS – why they are here. Who they have come for. When they will land. Two individuals say they were sent from the level above human and will return to that level in a spaceship (UFO) within the next three months. This man and woman will discuss how the transition from the human level to the next level is accomplished, and when this may be done . . . . If you have ever entertained the idea that there might be a real PHYSICAL level in space beyond the Earth's confines, you will want to attend this meeting.

More than human

Bo and Peep – formerly known as M.H. Applewhite and Bonnie Nettles – had convinced themselves that they were more than human, and had the strength of will and personality to maintain that impression; converts were clearly quite overwhelmed by them. At first they claimed that they would

one day be assassinated and then would be resurrected – after three days. Later these claims were set aside. As in other such groups, members were expected to make sacrifices: to give up their names and possessions, abandon the use of drugs, alcohol, radio and television, and not to indulge in sex – or even read books. The members generally lived in semi-permanent camps. The words of Bo and Peep in an interview recounted by Brad Steiger make their attitude to the family and other personal relationships clear:

> Husband and wife can take the trip at the same time – but not together. It would be impossible to become an individual if you went together on the trip . . . . In order to leave this Earth's atmosphere, you must go alone and overcome whatever needs you have for any other individual or thing of this Earth. Anything for which you depend on another human being or any thing on this Earth must be overcome.

Being a member of HIM was more like being a Moonie than participating in a traditional religion or even a traditional UFO cult. But the structure of the group was like that of other groups already described: there was a communicator, a message, a task.

No one has yet ascended to another physical realm above the atmosphere. Not many people seem to have got their money back, either. It turned out that Bo and Peep had met each other in a psychiatric hospital, where she was a nurse and he was a patient. Yet plenty of people remained willing to

Dragon Hill, near Uffington in Oxfordshire, is one of England's most mysterious ancient sites. It was recognised by two contactees, John and Sue Day, as the scene of dreams they had that seemed to foreshadow some future disaster for the world. UFOs figured in the dreams as saving a disease-ravaged remnant of the human race

believe them and to accept their discipline. Like so many fringe religions, it seems to have met spiritual needs shared by many people at the present time.

Let us look, finally, at one further vision of salvation by UFOs – one that has been experienced in dreams by Sue and John Day, an English couple. They claim to have been taken on board an alien spacecraft near the village of Aveley in Essex, England. In their dreams they saw a deep red Sun and a dark sphere hanging in a blood-coloured sky. Columns of weary men, women and children made their way through a devastated landscape towards the summit of a high hill.

There they waited for perhaps days, until their eyes caught the first glinting reflections from a formation of shining UFO-like craft appearing over the murky horizon, heading slowly in their direction. As they drew nearer a number of these craft broke away and descended over the hilltop, then began to lower ramps. The people seemed to know that at last 'they' had come. Come at last to take them away, away from the devastated planet Earth.

The Days identified the area in the dream as Dragon Hill, near Uffington. It seemed to them to be a presentiment of a possible, but avoidable, future – a future holding disaster, but also salvation for a fortunate few through the intervention of UFOs.

Reaching for the sky

Flying saucer cults may be no more than a haven for cranks – but is their interpretation of UFOs much odder than those of certain experts? This chapter compares some of the more exotic ideas entertained by ufologists

CULTS BASED ON UFO CONTACTEES have much in common – in their activities, in the way their leaders receive communications, and in the general tenor of those communications. But the specific claims made in the messages from 'space people' differ wildly from each other. The extra-terrestrials who guide them rarely even come from the same planet. However well-intentioned or warm-hearted the members of the groups may be, the divergences in their claims must lead the outsider to conclude that there is little reason to take them seriously. Whether or not the religious impulse that inspires them is authentic, the scientific trappings that they often don are distortions of valid science.

Yet the claims made by the cults are, if anything, less fantastic and disturbing than some of the theories that have been put forward by respected ufologists who have *not* surrounded themselves with followers and made claims to infallibility.

For example, although some of Brad Steiger's books should not be regarded as expressing his own opinions, the material in which his own attitude *can* be discerned seems to indicate a strong belief in the idea of

Above: UFOs descended on a French village in 1974 – but left no clue to their origin

Below: popular science writer Brad Steiger, who seems to believe that many historical figures were in touch with space beings

'Space Brothers' or 'Star People'. In one of his books the final chapter is contributed by his wife and is entitled 'How to contact multidimensional beings'. It states that 'Socrates, Napoleon, George Washington, Joan of Arc and Bernadette of Lourdes had contact with these beings.' Steiger himself has said:

> I am . . . convinced that there is a subtle kind of symbiotic relationship which exists between mankind and the UFO intelligences. I think that in some way, which we have yet to determine, they need us as much as we need them.

This begins to hint that mankind does not have control over its own destiny, but Steiger nevertheless believes that the higher beings with whom we are in contact are benevolent. Other writers have more frightening ideas. They believe that alien powers can control the experiences we have and the way we respond to them. Hypotheses of this kind are known as the 'control system theory', which is generally associated with Jacques Vallée:

> UFOs are the means through which man's concepts are being arranged. All we can do is to trace their effects on humans. . . . I suggest that it is human belief that is being controlled.

That is what Vallée wrote in *The invisible college*. He went further in *Messengers of deception*:

> I believe there is a machinery of mass

Above: D. Scott Rogo, whose account of UFOS includes the notion that the intelligence behind the phenomenon knows what humanity is thinking, and that contactees are 'the tools of a global plan'

manipulation behind the UFO phenomenon . . . UFO contactees are the tools of a global plan. These silent agents are walking among us unseen, placing social time bombs at strategic spiritual locations. Some fine morning we may wake up from our 'scientific' complacency to find strangers walking through the ruins of our Establishments.

Jerry Clark and D. Scott Rogo are a little plainer in their account:

Let's begin by supposing that somewhere in the universe there is an intelligence or force – we'll call it the Phenomenon for want of a better word – that's beaming projections of various kinds into our world. . . . Whatever its nature, it has some deep sense of what human beings are thinking, and it provides us with visions that reflect the concerns of the human mind.

Writing on his own account, Rogo has stated:
UFO abductions are physically real events. But they are dramas materialised into three-dimensional space for us by the Phenomenon. They are dreams that the Phenomenon made come to life in very frightening vividness. . . . Once someone has entered into psychic contact with the Phenomenon the link may become permanent, and reactivate periodically.

This is heady stuff, coming from figures of such stature and influence in the UFO field. But even Dr J. Allen Hynek, who has done so much to help make ufology respectable and acceptable on both sides of the Atlantic, has commented:

There are people who've had UFO experiences who've claimed to have developed psychic ability. There have been reported cases of healings in close encounters, and there have been reported cases of precognition, where people had foreknowledge or forewarning that they were going to see something. There has been a change of outlook, a change of philosophy in persons' lives. Now, you see, these are rather tricky things to talk about, but it's there.

Many people, like Jacques Vallée and I, to some extent, feel that it might be a conditioning process.

No hiding place
The control system theorists are not writing about occasional isolated incidents but about the worldwide evidence of a system to which mankind is bound and from which it cannot escape – a system that, they claim, existed before humanity appeared and will in turn outlive it.

John Keel's theories are perhaps the most terrifying of all. For him the control system, which he calls the Eighth Tower, is no longer running the show intelligently, but instead

The last days of the world

In *Messengers of deception* Jacques Vallée suggests that the UFO contactee cults are part of a sinister plan to undermine the power of rational thought for political

ends. While the desire to change the world is plain enough in the 'teachings' of contactees like Claude Vorilhon (left and, below, his book), will many people act on them?

Vorilhon claims to have been chosen by extra-terrestrials because he is French, from 'the country where democracy was born', but in order to survive the 'last days' of the present age we must 'eliminate elections and votes' and disband the military everywhere. The 'Elohim' – a Hebrew word meaning 'the gods' – will then return and give us the benefit of their wisdom.

The space people also gave him a new name and his peculiar insignia – a swastika set within the star of David. As if this were not enough, Vorilhon (now 'Rael') naïvely recounts other benefits of his position such as his romp in a bathtub with no less than five singularly lovely extra-terrestrial female robots! All this is told in the course of appealing for funds to build a mansion to house the Elohim when they return.

Do Vorilhon's simplistic and contradictory notions hold any political dangers? Probably not – but this century *has* seen far more irrational ideas turn into hideous reality.

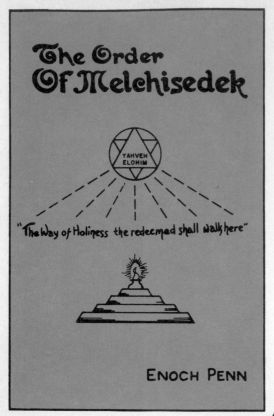

ENOCH PENN

Left: the cover of a book by Enoch Penn, a member of the now-defunct American religious sect, the Order of Melchisedek. From its writings it is clear that the group expected to gain earthly power, though the means to gain that power (among other things members were enjoined to refrain from orgasm, for example) were not calculated to gain it much popularity. Some of the ideas as well as the name of the sect have been taken over by contactee cults in the USA and elsewhere. The pentacle (below) was given to author Jacques Vallée by the French Melchisedek group

Below: Brad and Francie Steiger's book *Star people*, in which they discuss the presence of aliens on Earth and their plans for humanity

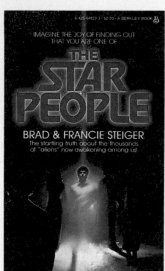

has gone out of control and is blindly following some preordained plan:

The human race has always been aware that it was serving as a pawn in some cosmic game. . . . We have been programmed well, but the Eighth Tower is dying of old age. The manifestations around us are not the work of the gods, but of a senile machine playing out the end game.

This implies that humanity has only the illusion of free will in the conduct of its affairs – a view more pessimistic than all but some extremely Calvinistic forms of traditional religion.

Certain Christian groups, particularly among the evangelical movements, have viewed the UFOs as sinister, though not as controlling human activity. The respected *Journal* of the Spiritual Counterfeits Project devoted an issue to UFOs and concluded thus:

Current UFO phenomena, insofar as they complete the patterns of fallen human speculation discussed earlier, while playing to that ignorant dynamism which drives us to the stars (to the neglect of our souls) cannot but be suspected of having their origin with Satan and his companions in spoilage and deceit. Add to this both the theological and statistical improbability that an extra-terrestrial race ever would (or could) visit Earth, and the odds lean greatly in favour of the possibility that UFOs *do* represent a visitation, but of extra*dimensionals* – demonic spirits which have gained the power to actually perform materialisations in the physical realm.

Setting Satan's stage

John Weldon and Zola Levitt, authors of a number of books on the paranormal written from a Christian viewpoint, have said:

Quite simply we think the demons are preparing the coming of the Antichrist. . . . To properly set the stage for the Antichrist, who really is a supernatural personality, the world has to be made ready to think in terms of the new and the strange. . . .

Meanwhile, an English clergyman, the Reverend Eric Inglesby, comments:

As psychic phenomena (which many UFOs are) the subject is interesting and potentially dangerous; in their spiritual aspect, involving the destiny of immortal souls, whether by false belief, or by spirit possession, or even by abduction, UFOs are not just dangerous – they are deadly. In some respects they are visible manifestations, to those who actually see them, of those principalities and powers which St Paul clearly identified as evil, not good.

Are UFOs as damaging as this mass of diverse opinion suggests? There is no convincing evidence to support the contention that they are physically or psychologically dangerous in a *direct* way: they cannot control our minds. But we can *make* UFOs dangerous to ourselves by bringing our own desires and fears to bear on the mass of recorded UFO data. Any of us can find material in that enormous accumulation to support our own personal opinions. The people who have created UFO contactee cults have built their own elaborate superstructures of belief.

We must regard the over-speculative interpretation of UFO data as a kind of temptation from which even the most intelligent, experienced and knowledgeable of commentators are not immune. The information we possess about UFOs makes a whole that is self-contradictory, confusing, outlandish and, often, incredible. We need to keep that simple fact in mind before building up our speculations on some selected part of the evidence.

The pattern of the future

How does one distinguish between prediction and prophecy? Can the concept of free will accommodate predestination? BRIAN INNES takes a look at the principal methods of divination, and begins with the ancient, but still flourishing, art of geomancy

'How now, you secret, black, and midnight hags!' Macbeth and Banquo encounter the Weird Sisters on a heath near Forres. The witches' prophecies were to change Macbeth's life, but they predicted nothing that did not remain in his control

THROUGHOUT THE HISTORY of mankind, those who were concerned about what the future held for them have sought guidance from 'wise' men and women. From the Azande tribesman who offers a chicken to the witch doctor in return for a prognostication of next month's weather, to the investor consulting his astrologer for assistance in forecasting future movements of the stock market, the motives, the means and the advice have always been very similar. But for all those prepared to *prophesy*, few would be prepared to say that they could *predict*.

The dangers inherent in placing too exact an interpretation on prophecy are exemplified very neatly in Shakespeare's *Macbeth*. Macbeth has – as the historian A.L. Rowse very rightly puts it – 'a flawed and ruined nobility – he is the victim of the Weird Sisters' prophecies; or, rather, of the promptings to which their "prophecies" gave confirmation.' In other words, Macbeth is given information that he interprets in one way; but subsequent events show that an entirely different, and equally plausible, interpretation could have been made.

When Macbeth first meets the witches, they hail him as thane of Cawdor, and as 'Macbeth, that shalt be king hereafter'. They also greet Banquo:

First Witch: Lesser than Macbeth, and greater.

Second Witch: Not so happy, yet much happier.

Third Witch: Thou shalt get kings, though thou be none . . .

Within minutes, Macbeth is named thane of Cawdor, and so, driven by ambition and the conviction that the witches have foretold his future, he murders King Duncan and himself becomes king of Scotland. Then, fearing that the rest of the witches' prophecy will also come true, he engineers the murder of Banquo – but Banquo's son Fleance escapes, and will sire a line of later kings.

But Macbeth must have more:

I will tomorrow,

And betimes I will, to the weird sisters:

More shall they speak; for now I am bent to know,

By the worst means, the worst.

The witches are only too happy to give Macbeth what he asks. They conjure up a succession of apparitions, who advise:

1. Beware Macduff.
2. None of woman born shall harm Macbeth.
3. Macbeth shall never be vanquished until Birnam wood comes to Dunsinane.
4. A line of kings shall follow Banquo's death.

Since he can do nothing about the last

prophecy, Macbeth determines to deal with the first. Learning that Macduff has already fled to England, he puts Lady Macduff and all her family to the sword. But he is greatly heartened by the other two prophecies, for they seem to imply clearly that no one shall harm him, and that he shall not be vanquished.

In the last scenes of the play, however, he discovers that the witches' words have another meaning. Birnam wood does indeed come to Dunsinane, for Malcolm's army wears its leafy branches as camouflage; and Macduff, who finally kills Macbeth, was not *born* of woman, but 'from his mother's womb untimely ripp'd' – that is, he was born by Caesarean section.

An inescapable fate?

Prophecy is the outcome of divination, and the example of Macbeth, and the advice given him by the witches, should serve to make clear the difference between divination and prediction. What the witches foretold was *not* predetermined: if Malcolm's men had not hidden behind leafy branches from Birnam wood, if Macduff had not returned from England to avenge the murder of his family, then Macbeth might well have lived out his reign and died in his own bed.

Indeed, Macbeth failed principally because of the psychological effect of the prophecies upon his self-confidence. The weird sisters did not make any specific predictions: they made only negative statements: 'None of woman born shall harm Macbeth. . .' and 'Macbeth shall never vanquished be until. . .'. They did not say that someone who was not born of woman *would* harm Macbeth; but the effect of their prophecy was that Macbeth's confidence was raised so high that, when he discovered that Macduff was not 'of woman born', he was immediately destroyed by his own guilt and superstitious fear.

If, then, divination is not prediction and is not concerned with predetermined events, what use is it? Why go to a fortune-teller with your problems, if a newspaper 'agony aunt' or even a close friend can provide you with a wealth of good advice? The reason, quite simply, is that the diviner does not make use of information that he or she consciously possesses about the person making the consultation: by the use of some means – whether it is the entrails of a freshly killed animal, arbitrarily chosen objects, a crystal ball, the astrological birth-chart of the subject or certain marks, such as moles, upon his person – the diviner is put in touch with information that is obtainable only by transcendental methods.

To those for whom a belief in the free will of the individual is paramount, the idea of a predetermined future is totally unacceptable. But look at it in this way. Someone's birth can be compared to the launching of a space vehicle. At the moment of 'lift-off', all

the conditions are known and understood by mission control: the rocket will follow a predetermined trajectory, and at a known time the vehicle will be detached and will follow a predetermined course. The astronaut need do nothing thereafter; he can leave the future manoeuvring of the vehicle to those on Earth. But he is also provided with manual controls that he can use himself; he may become bored and start tinkering with fine adjustments in flight that produce results he did not expect; or, in a fit of rage – or other show of temperament – he may throw himself about the capsule and disturb its equilibrium. Whatever he does, *of his own free will*, will be recorded by mission control; and they can immediately inform him what will be the outcome of his actions, however unplanned.

They can, however, only advise. If he persists in what he is doing he may miss his target and disappear for ever in the depths of space, and nothing that anybody on Earth can do will help him.

This is how divination works. The diviner can give advice on the basis of information that is not available to his subject; he can predict the outcome of a particular course of action and suggest an alternative; but he cannot state that any future event will definitely occur.

All divination, by whatever method, follows the same sequence:

First, a question is formulated. This may range from something very specific – such as 'Will I win today's lottery?' or 'Should I marry this man?' – to general enquiries of the form 'What will my future life be like?' Obviously, the more specific the question, the more specific the answer is likely to be – and, therefore, the more trustworthy it is for the enquirer. Generalised questions usually attract answers that are susceptible of many different interpretations.

Next, some physical means is employed to

Below: a geomancer practises his art. Reading meaning into randomly generated patterns remains popular. In the West, tea leaves are read, in other cultures the throwing of inscribed tablets – similar to the throwing of dice – is a common method of divination (divining tablets from Mashonaland, Zimbabwe, right). The belief persists that a specially gifted person – shaman, witch doctor or fortune teller (a Vietnamese stick thrower, below right) – is needed to practise divination, but it seems that almost anyone can

provide a link between the enquirer and the diviner. The enquirer may be asked to provide an intimate possession, to touch something belonging to the diviner, or to make an arbitrary choice of cards from a pack, objects thrown to the ground, or any random arrangement of things from which he does not make a conscious selection. Or the diviner may employ some device, such as a crystal ball or a pendulum, on which he can concentrate so intensely that consciousness of his surroundings recedes to a point where he is effectively in a trance. Drugs may also be used for this purpose.

Skill – or cunning?

Then, avoiding any temptation to make use of knowledge he may consciously possess about the enquirer, or to reason logically from one premise to another, the diviner *intuitively* produces his 'message'. Depending upon his skill – or cunning – this message may be straightforward advice of a practical nature, or a succession of cryptic statements that only the enquirer can interpret for himself. Frequently, as innumerable tales throughout history have told us, this advice can appear so obscure that the enquirer despairs of it; on occasion, diviners have been killed by their clients in an agony of frustration.

The methods of divination have their own archaic names, from abacomancy – divination from patterns of dust – to zoomancy – the observation of the behaviour of animals. There are, however, five methods of divination that have particularly attracted the attention of practitioners over the centuries, and that have therefore gathered about them a vast amount of literature and working tradition. These are astrology (see page 36), cartomancy, cheiromancy, geomancy, and the Chinese method of divination known as the *I Ching*.

Although astrology has claimed to be the oldest of these, there is little doubt that geomancy is as old – and it is certainly the

simplest. In this context, geomancy got its name from the practice of making a pattern of holes in the earth, and should not be confused with the Chinese practice of *feng-shui*, which is concerned with finding propitious places on which to erect tombs, build houses or found cities.

Geomancy, in fact, may be the surviving ancestor of the *I Ching*: the divinatory figures of geomancy are made up of four lines, and those of the *I Ching* of six. Since each line can take one of two forms, the total number of combinations in geomancy is only 16, compared with the 64 of the *I Ching*.

The lines may be marked in the dust or earth – which is how the art of geomancy got its name; or they may be made up of kernels or stones; or they may of course be marked on paper.

The art is said to have originated in Persia, but it is widespread over the whole of the Mediterranean region, the near East and much of Africa, and since its spread over this area followed the spread of Islam it is at least possible that Arab traders had brought it from China. In Malagasy, geomancy is known as *sikidi*; on the west coast of Africa as *djabe* or *fa*. In Europe, the first full description occurs in the second book of the *Occult philosophy* of Cornelius Agrippa (1531).

The right lines

The 'lines' from which the geomantic figure is derived can be obtained in a wide variety of ways. They may be straight horizontal lines traced – randomly and without conscious direction – in the dust, which are distinguished as short or long lines; or they may be either straight or wavy. These two classes of line are then identified as 'odd' or 'even', and are represented conventionally by either one or two stones, palm kernels or dots. Or the lines may be made up of a random succession of dots, the oddness or evenness being determined by the number of dots. In

fa, a handful of 18 palm kernels is passed from the left to the right hand, and the number of kernels remaining in the left hand is counted as either odd or even.

To make a geomantic figure, four lines are required. If, for instance, the first and third are even, and the second and fourth odd, the resultant figure will be:

Altogether, there are 16 of these figures, each with its own name and significance, as detailed in the accompanying table.

Below: how the geomantic figures are traditionally interpreted in the four main methods – the European, which uses Latin designations; the two West African systems of *fa* and *djabe*; and the *sikidi* of Malagasy

The meaning of the figures

Figure	Latin name	Fa	Djabe	Sikidi
	Puer Yellow; rash, inconsiderate	**Lete** Abscess	**Kaoussadji** Long Life	**Alakarabo** Leads to danger
	Amissio Loss	**Tche** Pearl	**Marili** Sickness	**Adalo** Tears; protection against enemies
	Albus White; wisdom	**Touloukpin** Unripe papaya fruit	**Baiala** Family	**Alohomora** Favourable to thieves
	Populus The crowd	**Yekou** Spirits of the dead	**Djamaha** The crowd	**Asombola** Plenty
	Fortuna major Good luck	**Houolin** Pointed shell	**Adouhi** Victory over an enemy	**Adabaray** Fire
	Conjunctio Joining together	**Holi** Removal of an obstacle	**Dam'hi** Success	**Alatsimay** Protects thieves and enemies
	Puella Girl; pretty face	**Toula** A firing gun	**Nagiha** Soon	**Alikisy** Good fortune in love; riches
	Rubeus Red; passion, vice	**Ka** Canoe	**Oumra** Marriage	**Alabiavo** Riches, jewels
	Aquisitio Success, gains, good fortune	**Fou** Blowing the fire	**Kali** Good fortune on the right; bad on the left	**Alihotsy** Lightness of spirit
	Carcer Prison, delay, confinement	**Di** Resistance	**Sikaf** Law, command	**Akikola** Protects vagabonds
	Tristitia Sorrow, melancholy	**Aklan** Porous stone	**Mankuss** Death	**Betsivongo** Obsession, tears
	Laetitia Joy, health, beauty	**Abla** Connection	**Laila** Riches	**Alahijana** Strength; happy marriage
	Cauda Draconis Exit, lower kingdom	**Gouda** Evil gods	**Sahili or Haridja** Serious intentions	**Karija** Fate
	Caput Draconis Entrance, upper kingdom	**Sa** Between the thighs	**Raia** Health	**Alakaosy** Evil fate, disputes, war
	Fortuna Minor Less good fortune; external aid	**Losso** Riven tree	**Sapari** Journeys	**Soralahy** Pride, domination
	Via The way, journeys	**Gbe** Language	**Dariki** Children	**Taraiky** Loneliness; death

In Africa, these figures are interpreted singly, or in pairs. In the European tradition, the procedure is more complicated. In the first operation 16 lines are produced, and these are used to generate four 'Mother' figures. Suppose for example that the four following Mothers are produced:

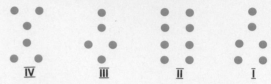

IV   III   II   I

These are respectively: Fortuna Minor, Populus, Puer and Conjunctio.

From these four Mothers four Daughters are produced, by adding the four lines horizontally, from right to left:

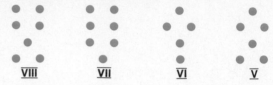

VIII   VII   VI   V

These are, respectively, Amissio, Puella, Tristitia and Albus.

Now four Nephews must be produced. The first Nephew is obtained by adding *together* the first and second Mothers, and marking the sum as before, with one dot for odd and two dots for even. So, from the first two Mothers, we get:

Fortuna minor

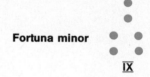

IX

And from the second two Mothers:

Puella

X

Similarly the third and fourth Nephews are formed by adding together the first and second, and the third and fourth, Daughters:

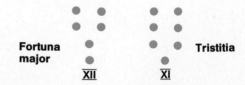

Fortuna major   XII   XI   **Tristitia**

From the Nephews, two Witnesses are obtained by the same process of adding together:

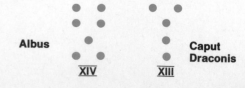

Albus   XIV   XIII   **Caput Draconis**

And finally, a Judge is obtained by adding together the lines of the two Witnesses:

Acquisitio

Right: a South African witch doctor casts and reads the 'wise stones'

The final pattern of 15 geomantic figures will provide the answer to one of 16 questions:

1. Will he have a long life?
2. Will he become rich?
3. Should he undertake the project?
4. How will the undertaking end?
5. Is the expected child a boy or a girl?
6. Are the servants honest?
7. Will the patient soon recover?
8. Will the lover be successful?
9. Will the inheritance be obtained?
10. Will the lawsuit be won?
11. Will he obtain employment?
12. How will he die?
13. Will the expected letter arrive?
14. Will the journey be successful?
15. Will good news arrive soon?
16. Will the adversary be overcome?

It can be seen that these questions cover most common preoccupations; with experience, the analysis of the geomantic pattern can be applied to other, rather more specific questions.

How are the figures interpreted, and how is the question answered? Let us suppose that the example above was obtained in answer to the question 'Will the lawsuit be won?'

In this case the Judge is Acquisitio, which signifies success, and the two Witnesses are Caput Draconis and Albus. These are all

Below: on the west coast of Africa, in the geomantic method known as *fa*, palm kernels are passed from hand to hand for a few moments. Those that end up in the left hand are counted and the geomantic figures are then formed from them

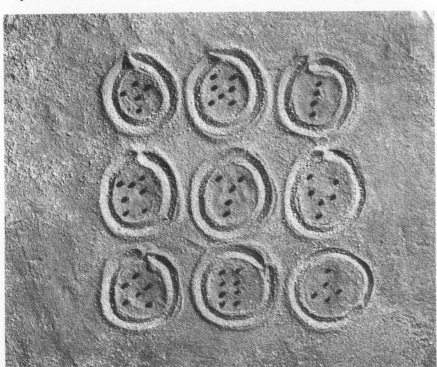

fortunate omens, and the implication is that wisdom will prevail and the lawsuit will be won with honour. We can investigate the progress of the lawsuit by considering the pattern of figures from the beginning. The outcome of the suit depends upon others (Fortuna Minor), whom we may suppose are the jury (Populus), likely to behave capriciously (Puer), but finally reaching a common verdict (Conjunctio). Perhaps the possibility of losing the suit (Amissio) is concerned with a girl (Puella), who can be the cause of sorrow (Tristitia) unless wisdom (Albus) prevails. The representative (Fortuna Minor) of the girl (Puella) could be a danger (Tristitia), but good fortune (Fortuna Major) will be the final outcome.

Open to interpretation

Geomancy is the most primitive of all the methods of divination, but this example shows clearly how adaptable it is as a means of interpretation. Because of the sequence of operations by which the Judges and Witnesses are obtained, there are only eight possible Judges – Acquisitio, Amissio, Fortuna Major, Fortuna Minor, Populus, Via, Conjunctio, Carcer – and each of these Judges has a possible eight combinations of Witness, this figure being doubled due to the fact that each Witness may stand on either right or left of the Judge. Altogether, therefore, there are 128 possible configurations of Judge and Witnesses, each of which can be an answer to one of 16 questions.

Methods of divination to be considered in succeeding chapters are far more complex. In the *I Ching*, for example, there are 64 basic figures; while in the use of the Tarot cards there are a minimum of 22 cards, which may be disposed in an almost infinite variety of ways.

I Ching: enquire within

One of the oldest and most flexible of divinatory methods is also the most fascinating. This chapter continues our discussion of divination with a brief look at the Chinese Book of Change

CONFUCIUS SAID: 'If some years were added to my life, I would give 50 to the study of the *I Ching*, and might then escape falling into great error.' That was in 481 BC, when he was already nearly 70 years old, and had written a series of commentaries on the text of the book the Chinese call *I Ching*, which means 'the Book of Change'.

The *I Ching* is one of the oldest and most respected oracle books in the world. In its present form it can be traced back at least 3000 years – and even at that time it was already considered venerable, being based upon more primitive forms of oracle.

The Book of Change draws its basic philosophy from the ancient Chinese faith known as Tao. The word 'tao' is most usefully translated as 'way' – as in the Christian expression 'I am the Way, the

Far right: K'ung Fu-tzu, the great Chinese philosopher known to us as Confucius

Below: a romanticised Western view of the ceremony involved in consulting the I Ching: the sticks are being passed through the smoke from an incense burner, while the enquirer makes his kowtows before them

Truth, the Life' – but no English word provides a really satisfactory equivalent, and even in Chinese it is susceptible of a variety of meanings. Indeed, as one Chinese inscription puts it: 'the Tao that can be put into words is not Everlasting Tao.'

Taoist writings are full, in fact, of negative definitions: 'power and learning is adding more and more to oneself, Tao is subtracting day by day; rigour is death, yielding is life; as laws increase, crimes increase.'

To the Taoist sage the world is not made up of discrete particles of time and space: everything is part of everything else, and reality consists of ceaseless change. The river that one paddled in yesterday is not the river one swims in today; and so the Universe is seen as a moving pattern in which nothing is permanent. So the *I Ching* is different from other oracle books: it does not regard the past, the present and the future as fixed; instead, it treats time and fate as dynamic and flowing, never the same from one moment to the next. The advice that one obtains by consulting the *I Ching*, therefore, is of possibilities: if you act in a particular way it is likely to result in such-and-such an outcome.

As a tool of divination, the *I Ching* is very similar to geomancy in principle (see page 19); but the divinatory figures that are generated are composed of six lines instead of four, and therefore there are a possible 64, rather than 16, figures. Moreover, where the

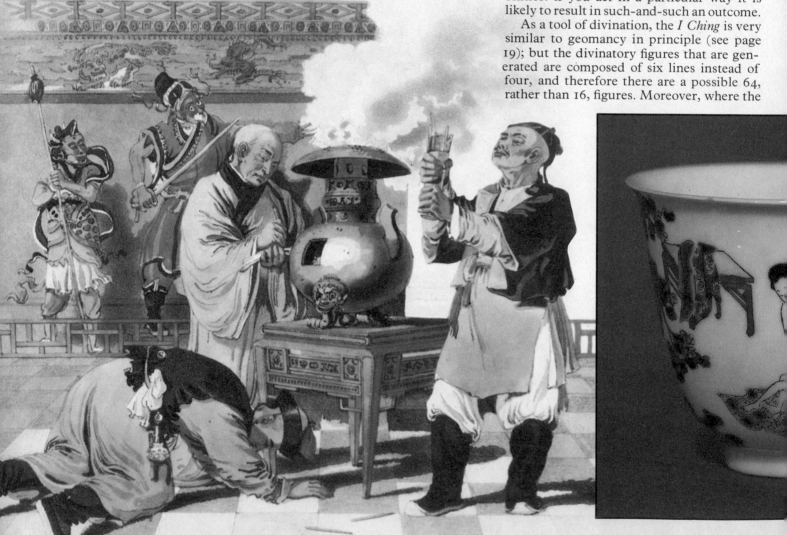

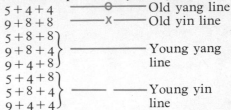

Witness-Judge procedure of geomancy results in only 128 different interpretations, each of the *I Ching* figures contains within itself 64 possible variations, and can generate at least one further figure: the total number of interpretations, therefore, is:

$$64 \times 64 + 64 = 4160.$$

Taoist philosophy classifies all the energies of the Universe under two headings, yin and yang. Yin is passive, watery, pertaining to the Moon, essentially female; yang is active, fiery, pertaining to the Sun, essentially male. The lines that make up the divinatory figures are described as either yin or yang lines; a broken line represents yin, a continuous line yang.

The six-line figures are known as hexagrams. Each can be regarded as made up of two three-line figures called trigrams. Since each line of each trigram can be either continuous or broken, the number of trigrams is $2 \times 2 \times 2 = 8$. And since each hexagram is made up of two trigrams, the number of hexagrams is $8 \times 8 = 64$.

The traditional way in which these figures are generated is long and complicated. A bundle of 50 dried yarrow stalks is required; yarrow was used because it had a certain holy significance to the Chinese. One of the stalks is set aside, and is not used in obtaining the hexagram; there is some dispute among Western writers as to whether the fiftieth stalk plays any part in the tradition of the *I Ching* or not.

The remaining 49 stalks are then separated into two piles. After this, the procedure is as follows:

1. One stalk from the right-hand pile is placed between the little finger and ring finger of the left hand.
2. Stalks are removed four at a time from the left-hand pile until four or less are left. These stalks are placed between the ring finger and the middle finger of the left hand.
3. Stalks are removed four at a time from the right-hand pile until four or less are left. These stalks are placed between the middle finger and the index finger of the left hand.

The stalks held between the fingers of the left hand will now total either 5 or 9:

$$1 + 1 + 3 = 5$$
$$\text{or } 1 + 3 + 1 = 5$$
$$\text{or } 1 + 2 + 2 = 5$$
$$\text{or } 1 + 4 + 4 = 9$$

These stalks are then put aside, and the process is repeated with the remaining 40 or 44 stalks. At the end, the stalks held between the fingers will total either 4 or 8:

$$1 + 1 + 2 = 4$$
$$\text{or } 1 + 2 + 1 = 4$$
$$\text{or } 1 + 4 + 3 = 8$$
$$\text{or } 1 + 3 + 4 = 8$$

This pile is also set aside, and the process repeated with the remaining stalks. Once more, the stalks held in the left hand will total either 4 or 8.

There are now three little piles: the first contains 5 or 9 stalks, the second and third each contain 4 or 8. There are therefore eight possible combinations of these three quantities. These provide a yin or yang line:

$5 + 4 + 4$	—⊖— Old yang line
$9 + 8 + 8$	—✗— Old yin line
$\left.\begin{array}{l}5 + 8 + 8 \\ 9 + 8 + 4 \\ 9 + 4 + 8\end{array}\right\}$	——— Young yang line
$\left.\begin{array}{l}5 + 4 + 8 \\ 5 + 8 + 4 \\ 9 + 4 + 4\end{array}\right\}$	— — Young yin line

The 'old' lines are also known as 'moving' lines: an Old yang line is seen to be changing into a Young yin line, and an Old yin line into a Young yang line. Each of the four types of line is also given a 'ritual number':

Old yin line	6
Young yang line	7
Young yin line	8
Old yang line	9

So far, only a single line has been generated. This is drawn as the bottom line of the hexagram, and then the procedure must be repeated five times more, the lines being drawn in ascending order.

Producing a single hexagram, therefore, can take five minutes or more. Those who let the *I Ching* govern their lives have developed a simpler and quicker method that requires only three coins. Chinese coins traditionally had an inscribed face and a blank or 'reverse' face – the side of a modern coin that gives the value is considered the inscribed side: if the blank face is given the value 3, and the inscribed face the value 2, tossing the three coins will provide a total of 6, 7, 8 or 9 – and so, taking this as the ritual number, the first line is obtained. It is possible, in this way, to obtain the hexagram in less than a minute.

What follows the obtaining of the hexagram? The texts of the *I Ching* are of several different periods and different kinds. First comes a description of the hexagram itself, in terms of the two trigrams of which it is composed; then comes the Judgement, which is said to have been composed by King Wen, the founder of the Chou dynasty (*c.*1100 BC). This is a rather brief analysis of the hexagram as a whole.

'The superior man'

The next text, the Commentary, is traditionally attributed to Confucius, although it is improbable that he himself wrote it. This is generally longer than the Judgement, and takes note of the significance of the individual lines making up the whole hexagram. The third text, the Image, is succinct; it describes the kind of action that the sensible person – referred to usually as 'the superior man' – should take. This text has also been attributed to Confucius.

The final group of texts were composed by King Wen's son, the Duke of Chou, who destroyed the Shang dynasty in 1027 BC. These were written about 40 years after Wen's text: they are brief and rather cryptic, and they deal with the occurrence of Old

Below: the philosophy of Tao contains a strong sexual element, and intercourse is regarded as the interchange of yin and yang between the two partners. The cup represents Autumn Days, the last of the Thirty Heaven and Earth postures: 'The lord Yang lies on his back, his hand at the back of his head, and lady Yin sits on his stomach, but turning her face to his feet'

yang and yin lines within the hexagram.

One or two specific examples will illustrate the nature of these different texts, and the way in which they are interpreted.

In hexagram 63, Chi Chi – Climax and After – the upper trigram is K'an, which symbolises dangerous deep water, the Moon, the winter season, the north, the middle son, an ear, the 'element' wood and the colour red; the lower trigram is Li, representing fire, the Sun, summer, the south, the middle daughter, the eye, and the colour yellow.

The text of *I Ching* describes Chi Chi as being an evolutionary phase of hexagram 11, T'ai, which means Peace. Hexagrams are read from the bottom, and the 'strong' positions are considered to be lines 1, 3 and 5. In T'ai, lines 1, 2 and 3 are occupied by yang lines, while lines 4, 5 and 6 are yin; in Chi Chi, the yang lines have migrated upward to their appropriate positions, displacing the yin lines to position 2, 4 and 6. Thus, says the text, everything is in its proper place. But although this is a very favourable hexagram, it still gives grounds for caution: for it is when equilibrium has been reached that any sudden displacement may cause order to revert to disorder.

The Judgement on Chi Chi reads: 'After the climax there is success in small matters. Righteous persistence brings its reward. Good fortune in the beginning, but disorder in the end.'

Now comes the Commentary. 'Chi Chi indicates progress in small matters. The proper position of the yang and yin lines shows that righteous persistence will be rewarded; the weak line at the centre of the lower trigram indicates good fortune in the beginning, but the way peters out, efforts come to an end, and disorder returns.' This is one of a number of cases in which the Commentary seems to add very little to the Judgement, but in other cases it can be of considerable value in elucidating the often obscure phrases of the Judgement.

The verses of the Duke of Chou refer to the occurrence of 'moving' lines, the Old yang and Old yin lines. The bottom line of Chi Chi is a yang line: if it is an Old yang line, with a ritual number 9, then the verse for that line should also be read.

These Old lines are also moving into Young lines. Suppose, for instance, that the hexagram Chi Chi was obtained as follows:

When the old lines have changed into their opposites, the hexagram will be:

This is a very different hexagram. It is 62,

63 Chi Chi Climax and After

The trigrams:
above: K'an dangerous deep water
below: Li fire, brightness
This hexagram represents an evolutionary phase of hexagram 11, T'ai, Peace. The strong yang lines have moved upward into their appropriately strong positions, displacing the yin lines into their proper weak positions. Everything is in its proper place. But although this is a very favourable hexagram, it still gives grounds for caution: for it is when equilibrium has been reached that any sudden movement may cause order to revert to disorder.

The Judgement
After the climax there is a success in small matters. Righteous persistence brings its reward. Good fortune in the beginning, but disorder in the end.

Commentary
Chi Chi indicates progress in small matters. The proper position of the yang and yin lines shows that righteous persistence will be rewarded; the weak line at the centre of the lower trigram indicates good fortune in the beginning, but the way peters out, efforts come to an end, and disorder returns.

The Image
Water over the fire, the image of Chi Chi.

The superior man, accordingly, gives due thought to the misfortunes to come, and takes precautions in advance.

The Lines
In the bottom line, NINE signifies:
Like a driver who brakes his chariot,
Or a fox with a wet tail.
No blame.

In the second line, SIX signifies:
She loses her carriage curtain.
Do not run after it.
For in seven days it will be recovered.

In the third line, NINE signifies:
The Illustrious Ancestor
The emperor Wu Ting
Attacked the country of devils.
Three years he took in subduing it.
Small men are not fit for such enterprises.

In the fourth line, SIX signifies:
The finest clothes turn to rags.
Be careful all day long.

In the fifth line, NINE signifies:
The neighbour in the east sacrifices an ox:
But it is the neighbour in the west,
With his small spring sacrifice,
Who is blessed for his sincerity.

In the sixth line, SIX signifies:
His head is in the water.
Misfortune.

Hsiao Kuo. The Judgement, Commentary and Image for this second figure should also be read for interpretation, but since the lines have now moved the verses of the Duke of Chou are not significant.

One can go further: if the lines are moving independently of one another, there are two possible intermediate hexagrams between Chi Chi and Hsiao Kuo. These are:

The first is 49, Ko; the second is 39, Cheng. Reading the texts for these two hexagrams, but remembering that only one can be the true intermediate, may help in the interpretation.

One has to be very careful in trying to present an imaginary worked example of the use of the *I Ching*: too often, indeed, one finds that the hexagram obtained is Meng:

> I do not seek out the inexperienced; he comes to find me. When he first asks my advice, I instruct him. But if he comes a second or a third time, that is troublesome, and I do not advise the troublesome. . . .

As an experiment, I asked the *I Ching* 'whether it would be wise for me to finish this chapter tonight'. The hexagram I obtained was 20, Kuan:

Kuan signifies contemplation: 'the worshipper who has washed his hands, but not yet made the offering'. The upper trigram of Kuan is Sun, representing wind and gentleness; the lower trigram is K'un, the Earth, the passive. The Image of Kuan is the wind moving over the Earth. 'So did the kings of old visit all parts of their kingdom, to see their people and give them instruction.'

There is an Old yin line in the second line, which signifies:

> Contemplation through the crack of the door
> Is sufficient only for a housewife

and the Old yang line in the sixth line signifies:

> Contemplating himself
> The superior man is without reproach.

It seems that *I Ching* is advising me not to continue with the chapter until I have had time to think about it some more; it also suggests that my time would be better occupied in assertaining whether the editorial staff have any problems.

Now the moving lines must be allowed to develop, and the resultant hexagram is 29, K'an:

This is one of only eight hexagrams in which the trigram is doubled. In each trigram a strong yang line has plunged into the deep between two yin lines, as water lies in a deep ravine. The Judgement reads: 'Abyss upon abyss, danger piled on danger. But if you are sincere there is success locked up within.' The Commentary continues the theme, and the Image of K'an is: 'The water flows on and on to its destination; the image of the abyss upon the abyss. So the superior man walks in eternal virtue, instructing others in the conduct of their affairs.'

The last part of this text clearly relates to the advice given above – although the warnings of danger seem unnecessarily strong in such a minor matter. Can the intermediate hexagrams throw any light on the matter?

The two possible intermediates are:

These are, respectively, 59, Huan, and 8, Pi.

Huan signifies dispersal, and the advantageousness of travel. In the sixth line, the Old yang line signifies:

> He disperses bloodiness
> Keeping evil at a distance
> Departing without blame.

Pi, on the other hand, is the image of holding together; it signifies those who follow the lead of the superior man.

It was only a light-hearted question, and it deserves a light-hearted answer. The *I Ching* has told me that it is time for me, and my staff, to stop work and go home!

Is it possible to read an individual's future from a pack of Tarot cards? This chapter describes the most popular method of divination, explaining how the cards are consulted and how the significance of each one can be interpreted

THE DIVINATORY methods so far considered are aleatory – that is, they are based upon what seems to be a random selection of identical elements. The word 'aleatory' comes from the Latin for dice-player, and of course one of the simplest of divinatory methods consists in the throwing of one or two dice.

However, numerous experiments in psychokinesis have suggested that an experienced dice-thrower can influence the results of his play; and it may well be that the subconscious mind, or some transcendental aspect of it, is able to calculate the implications of the number of geomantic marks being made, or, as in the *I Ching*, yarrow stalks selected, before the hand has completed its movements.

It is certainly worth postulating that the mind, being in some kind of telepathic awareness of all the interpretations available, in some way selects the most suitable answer

Coming up trumps

to the question that has been posed, and then subconsciously causes the appropriate figure to be generated.

Some process of this kind seems to be at work in divination by means of the Tarot pack, which is probably nowadays the most popular of all methods.

The use of a pack of cards for divination is definitely not aleatory, since each of the elements selected is distinct, and has a particular significance all its own. There are a number of packs of specially designed cards available for divination – the French firm of Grimaud, for example, market such sets as the cards of 'Mademoiselle Le Normand', or 'The Parlour Sybil' – but most diviners are able to make do with an ordinary pack of playing cards. And in this respect it is important to remember that the Tarot pack is also an *ordinary pack of playing cards.* Although some of the images of the Tarot pack may appear bizarre to north-western Europeans familiar only with the standard 52-card bridge and whist pack, they do not embody an intrinsic occult significance. For 500 years, the Tarot cards have been the standard pack for a variety of common card games that go under the generic name of *tarok* or *tarocchi.*

There are very many ways of 'consulting the cards', and there is no reason to suppose that any one way is more correct or successful than any other. All that is important is that the practitioner should be completely confident about his or her method and the way in which the cards are to be interpreted. The easier methods make use only of the 22 trumps, which have been given by occultists the impressive title of Greater Arcana; the distinctive images of these cards are of great help in attaching significance to each, and in remembering what that significance is.

More complicated methods employ all 78 cards; but here even experienced practitioners find it necessary to resort to textbooks to remind them of the accepted significance of the numbered suit cards.

Ideally, to make consulting the Tarot a true divinatory method, each practitioner should decide exactly what meaning to attach to each card – even if this departs widely from what is commonly held to be the meaning, it should not affect the process of divination in any way. In practice, it is common to consult a textbook on the subject; although this may provide a rather stilted, formalised interpretation, it makes divination by Tarot very much easier.

The same kind of divinatory process can of course be carried out with a pack devoid of

The first mention of playing cards occurs in records for the years 1377 to 1379; by the end of the 15th century (above) they were widespread in Europe

Opposite: stages in the development of the images of two representative Tarot cards, Strength (above) and The Fool (below). The packs represented are, respectively: one attributed to Bonifacio Bembo, executed about 1480 (left); the 'Swiss' pack published by Müller since the late 18th century (centre top); a modern Italian pack of traditional design published by Modiano (centre); the Grimaud 'Marseilles' pack, from a 17th-century design (centre bottom); pack designed by the occultist Oswald Wirth, late 19th century (top right); a Spanish pack of early 20th century design (centre right); and pack designed by another occultist, A.E. Waite, and published at the turn of the century (bottom right)

Tarot trumps, such as a common 52 or 56 card pack, but in this case the interpretation is commensurately more difficult.

The ways in which the cards are used in divination are of two kinds: either a select number of cards is chosen for interpretation, or the complete pack is disposed according to a formula, producing a pattern of distribution in which the position of the card determines its part in the divinatory process.

As in all other methods of divination, the process comprises a questioner, who asks for advice by proposing a particular question, and the diviner, who interprets the answer. The cards may be dealt out either by the questioner or by the diviner – no two authorities agree on this, and it may also depend upon the particular method employed – but it is essential that both should concentrate fully upon the question. As with the *I Ching*, a frivolous question, or one that is idly put, will provoke an answer that may be equally facetious or, possibly, quite frightening in its implications.

One example must suffice to show how the Tarot cards are laid out in a pattern, and how they are then used for divination.

The questioner in this case is a mature but

still young woman, who has been married for several years; she has a full-time professional job. Due partly to the tastes and partly to the particular ambitions of her husband, she finds herself compelled to live in a district that she finds unpleasant. Should she endeavour to make her present home as pleasant as possible, or should she try to persuade her husband to move elsewhere?

The particular arrangement of cards used is one known as the 'Celtic cross'; only the 22 Tarot trumps are required for this.

1. A card is chosen to represent the question; this is known as the significator. In this particular case The Star, representing 'new beginning; pleasure; salvation', was the card selected.

2. The questioner shuffles the remaining cards, cuts them, and places them in a pile some way to the left of the significator.

3. The top card of the pile is turned over from left to right (so that it remains as it was in the pile, either upright or reversed) and placed directly on top of the significator. This card represents the present conditions in which the questioner lives or works. The card is The World. In spite of the nature of the question asked, it therefore would appear that the questioner is on the whole satisfied

change; it brings knowledge of the future and new understanding of the past; it advises the questioner to face up to whatever change may come.

These first six cards drawn have presented a picture of the questioner and her problem, as well as revealing some small details that she did not provide. The final four cards, which are placed one above the other to the right of the table, supply the divinatory advice.

1. The first card represents the present position of the questioner, and may answer the question directly. It is Death – not to be taken literally, for this card represents change by transformation.

2. The second card represents people and factors that may have an influence upon the answer. It is the Wheel of Fortune which, though it also signifies change, counsels prudence.

3. The third card reveals the inner feelings of the questioner, which she may well have kept hidden. It is the Moon, reversed; this suggests very strongly that the questioner does not really want to make the change that she has said she is considering.

4. The final card represents the end result of everything indicated by the preceding cards. The Pope is the representative of the firm foundations of our lives, the concepts of natural law and justice. This card, appearing in this position, suggests that the questioner and her husband have a mutual sympathy and understanding; their marriage appears to be a successful one; and it would be dangerous to threaten its stability by pursuing the change that was the subject of the question.

The account book of the treasurer to Charles VI of France records a payment in the year 1392 to the painter Jacquemin Gringonneur for three packs of cards 'in gold and various colours, of several designs, for the amusement of the said King'. The three cards illustrated here – Death (left), The Sun (right) and The Fool (below right) – are from 17 that survive in the Bibliothèque Nationale in Paris and that were long believed to be the original Gringonneur cards. They are now, however, thought to be from the 15th century and of Italian origin

with her lot, and feels a sense of achievement in her work, and perhaps also in her home.

4. The second card is placed across the first, to represent any immediate influences that may affect the interests of the questioner. The card is Temperance: whatever decision is reached, it is likely to be controlled by reason.

5. The third card is placed above the first group of cards, to represent the ultimate aim of the questioner. This is the Fool, reversed, which confirms the previous card. And since it is reversed, it signifies the opposite of luck or fate, and implies a rational outcome.

6. The fourth card is placed below the first group to represent the influences from the past that have affected the questioner and the question she asks. The Empress tells us that she is a woman of considerable understanding and intuition.

7. The fifth card is placed to the right of the central group to represent the recent past. The Hermit suggests that the passage of time has brought wisdom and further understanding.

8. The sixth card is placed to the left of the central group to represent influences that may come into play in the near future. The Hanged Man represents adaptability and

A brief summary of the symbolic significance of the Tarot trumps	
1 Magician	Man in search of knowledge; the answer he seeks
2 Woman Pope	Intuition, inspiration; subconscious memory, lack of foresight
3 Empress	Human understanding, femininity, sensuality, beauty and happiness
4 Emperor	Masculinity, independence, creativity, action
5 Pope	Advice: justice; healing
6 Lovers	Choice, decision
7 Chariot	Achievement, success; danger of defeat
8 Justice	Caution in taking advice; control of one's fate
9 Hermit	Time; wisdom; withdrawal
10 Wheel of Fortune	Change; prudence; the eternal return
11 Fortitude	Strength of purpose, coming danger
12 Hanged Man	Adaptability; desire to learn; violent change and sacrifice
13 Death	Change by transformation, rebirth
14 Temperance	Moderation, mercy; modification
15 Devil	The adversary; caution
16 The Tower	Punishment; pride; divine inspiration
17 The Star	New beginning; pleasure; salvation
18 The Moon	Uncertainty; changeability
19 The Sun	Splendour, health, wealth, affection; treachery
20 Judgement	Punishment or reward; final achievement
21 The World	Fulfilment, completion on a material level
0 The Fool	Fate; luck; the end

Above: how the Tarot cards are laid out in the spread known as the 'Celtic cross'. The significator card is The Star; laid on top of this is The World, representing the present condition of the questioner, and Temperance lies across both. Subsequent interpretation is explained in the text

A pattern of Tarot cards, however many have been laid out, is obviously very different from the pattern of dots obtained in geomancy (see page 19), or the pattern of lines in the *I Ching* (see page 24). Each of the cards has its own significance, and the position of each in the pattern also has a particular meaning. The Tarot cards must be read like the pages of a book: if we consider only the 22 trumps, there are over a thousand million million million different sequences. Add to this the incalculable number of groups of two, three, four or more and you will see that a combination can be obtained that will represent every conceivable situation – and that still leaves another 56 cards that can be used in interpretation

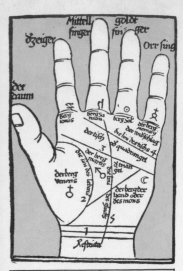

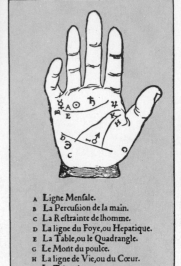

A Ligne Menfale.
B La Percuffion de la main.
C La Reftrainte de lhomme.
D La ligne du Foye, ou Hepatique.
E La Table, ou le Quadrangle.
G Le Mont du poulce.
H La ligne de Vie, ou du Cœur.
I Le Triangle.
K La ligne Moyenne naturelle.

On the other hand...

The lines of the hand are as individual as personality – but is there a connection between them? And can a diviner trace a person's destiny in his or her palm? This chapter examines the practice of palmistry, still widely popular as a form of divination

DIVINATION IS a means of answering questions and giving advice on what future action should be undertaken by the questioner. It works best with intense concentration of both practitioner and questioner, apparently by providing some kind of telepathic insight into the nature of the problem, the personality of the questioner, and the probable outcome of any given action.

To obtain the necessary concentration, almost all practitioners require some object on which they can focus their conscious faculties, in order to give the subconscious a free rein. Certain practitioners make use of something like a crystal ball, or a pendulum; but greater success seems to be achieved if the object on which attention is focused has some direct physical relationship with the questioner: playing cards that have been shuffled and cut by him or her, or some other kind of object that has been handled.

So far, all the methods of divination described in these chapters – geomancy (see page 19), the *I Ching* (see page 24) and the Tarot (see page 28) – have required a

personal involvement on the part of the questioner, but the means of divination has always been physically divorced from him or her. There remains one major divinatory method that requires the closest co-operation of the questioner, because the object being consulted is part of the human body itself. This method is cheiromancy, more popularly known as palmistry.

There are many who would not regard palmistry as a divinatory method at all. Since the law recognises the uniqueness of the human fingerprint, there is every reason to suppose that the palmprint is just as individual. We recognise a particular dog or cat

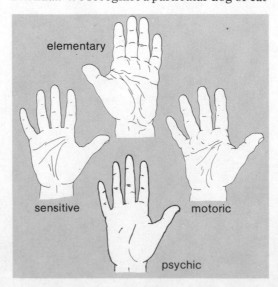

elementary

sensitive

motoric

psychic

Above left: palmistry has a long and venerable history – and remains popular today

Top: a diagram from Bartolomeo Cocle and (above) from Jean d'Indagine illustrating the ancient association between parts of the hand and the planets

Left: the four basic shapes of the hand according to Carl Carus. The 'elementary' hand is typical of the manual worker; the 'motoric' is large and strong but flexible, and is found among businessmen and craftsmen; the 'sensitive' hand, typical of writers and artists, is not as strong as the 'motoric' but is full of energy; and the 'psychic' is long and soft, indicating a personality that is sensitive and intuitive

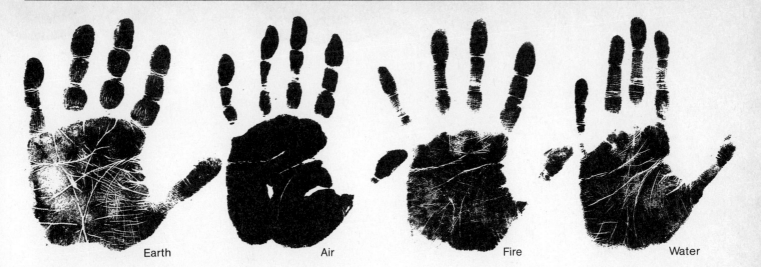

Earth   Air   Fire   Water

by the distinctive pattern of its coat, and we could similarly recognise a person by the pattern of their palmprint. Since it is well-known that animal coat patterns are affected by many factors – the climate, the time of year, the health and genetic background of the individual – it is at least arguable that the human palmprint similarly has something to tell us about the individual.

One palmist, in fact, has claimed that he read a young man's hand, saw that there was a strong indication that he might commit suicide, and suggested to him that he should have psychiatric help – and that six months later the lines of the young man's hand had changed out of all recognition.

There is some scientific evidence that the occurrence of abnormal lines on the hands may be related to certain hereditary diseases, such as heart defects or those related to chromosome deficiencies. In traditional palmistry the so-called 'simian' line – in which the Head line and the Heart line run as one – is held to be an indicator of 'degeneracy'; now a group of doctors in New York has reported that this line often occurs in mongoloid children or in those whose mother suffered an attack of rubella (German measles) during pregnancy.

Above: the 'Earth' hand is square, with short strong fingers and few lines; the 'Air' hand has longer fingers and finer lines; the fingers of the 'Fire' hand are short with many lines; and the 'Water' hand is narrow and delicate, with a mesh of fine lines

Below: the 'elementary' hand is typical of primitive people; the 'square' hand indicates a practical nature; the 'spatulative' hand denotes excitability; the 'philosophic' hand is self-explanatory; the 'conic' hand indicates someone who prefers pleasure to work; the 'psychic' hand speaks for itself. But most hands fall into the 'mixed' category

Right: the mounts and fingers

Whether or not there is any validity in this suggestion of a direct connection between the human metabolism and the lines of the hand, there is no doubt that the commonly accepted significance of the lines and parts of the hand must be based upon many centuries of empirical observation. Cheiromancy is recognised in the Bible, as in Proverbs 3:16: 'Long life is given in her right hand. In her left are riches and honour.' Or in Job 37:7: 'He seals up the hand of every man, that all men may know his work.'

Indeed, in this second verse, we can detect the old magical element in cheiromancy, the belief 'as above, so below'. It is quite possible that the first palmists believed the lines of the hand to be some sort of map of celestial motion, rather as if the subject's horoscope had been printed there.

But whatever credence we may give to the interpretations placed upon individual lines

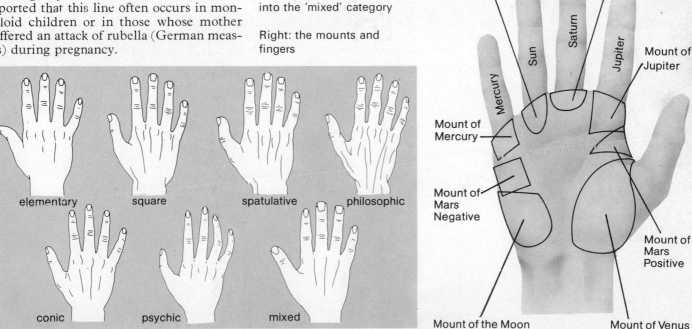

elementary   square   spatulative   philosophic

conic   psychic   mixed

Mount of the Sun   Mount of Saturn

Mercury   Sun   Saturn   Jupiter

Mount of Jupiter

Mount of Mercury

Mount of Mars Negative

Mount of Mars Positive

Mount of the Moon   Mount of Venus

of the hand, there are other tenets of palmistry that are borne out by both popular and medical belief. Palmists place great importance on the form of the whole hand: its shape, its moistness or dryness, its relative fleshiness, the length and shape of the fingers, and the relationship of the thumb and fingers to the palm. And isn't this just what we all do – even subliminally – when we judge an individual's personality, and even the state of their health, from the touch of their hands?

There are a number of different methods

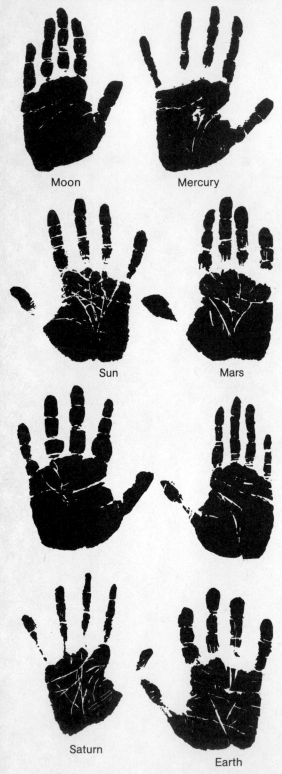

Moon   Mercury

Sun   Mars

Saturn

Earth

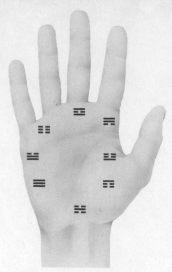

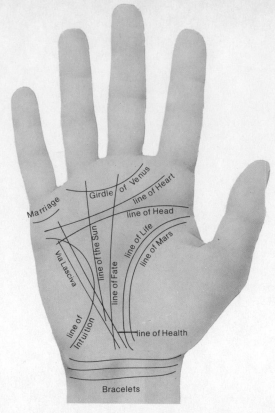

Above: the eight 'Palaces' of the hand in the Chinese system. Clockwise from the Mount of the Moon, these are: Ch'ien, for spiritual force; Tui, for sexual delight; K'un, for passivity; Li, for social and financial standing; Sun, for mental capacity; Chen, for energy and vitality; Ken, for obstinacy; and K'an, for difficulties to be faced

Above right: lines of the hand according to present-day practice

Left: classification of hand shapes on astrological principles. The Lunar hand is soft, with many lines: it indicates a restless but easygoing nature. The Mercurial hand, with its long finger of Mercury, denotes intellectual ability and quick wits. The Solar hand, with strong, short fingers, indicates ambition and trustworthiness. The Venusian hand, with its prominent Mount of Venus, is a sign of a cheerful and extrovert personality. The Martial hand has a very developed thumb and denotes courage and energy. The Jupiterian hand, with its thick and heavy fingers, is a sign of even temper and generosity. A long finger of Saturn characterises the Saturnine hand, indicating patience and shrewdness. The Earth hand is thick and firm, denoting a generous, slow but sure personality – and a loyal friend

of classification of the basic shape of the hand. The German Carl Carus proposed four types, which he named 'elementary', 'motoric', 'sensitive' and 'psychic'; the Frenchman Casimir d'Arpentigny increased this to seven, the 'elementary', 'square' (or 'useful'), 'spatulative' (or 'necessary'), 'philosophic', 'conic', (or 'artistic'), 'psychic' and 'mixed' hands.

Under the pseudonym of le Comte de St Germain, a late-19th-century writer expanded these to 14, including such oddities as the Congenital Idiot's hand and the Brutal Murderer's hand. In the 20th century, however, the tendency has been to reduce the number of shapes once more to four; a popular classification has been into Earth, Air, Fire and Water hands.

Astrological magic

Classifications of this kind have a certain natural logic to them; it is when we come to the fingers and the 'mounts' of the hand that astrological magic begins to take over. The mounts are the fleshy areas of the hand around the central palm, and each, with its related finger, is associated with one of the planets.

It is interesting to note that the fourth finger, which is associated with Apollo or the Sun, was long believed to have a vein running through it that connected directly to the heart, and it is for this reason that wedding rings are always placed upon this finger.

And so we come to the very complicated markings that appear all over the palm, the wrist and the fingers, and that no two people possess identically. There has been a great deal of argument among palmists as to the relative significance of the lines on left and right hands respectively, which can differ quite markedly. The commonest (and perhaps the most sensible) theory is that, in a right-handed person whose lines will obviously be affected by the work they do throughout their lives, the lines of the left hand represent the destiny to which they were born, and the lines of the right hand represent what they have made of their life.

The lines of the palm are divided into principal and subsidiary lines. The 15th-century writer Jean d'Indagine recognised only four principal lines: the mensal, or line of Fortune; the line of Life, or line of Heart; the Middle line, which represented the subject's career; and the line of Liver, or Health line.

Indagine's near-contemporary, Bartolomeo Cocle, added a further line, the line of Fate, running from the wrist direct to the finger of Saturn; and later 17th-century

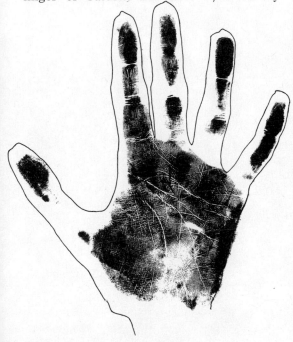

writers identified more lines according to our modern nomenclature.

The subsidiary lines, which do not appear on every hand, are the Girdle of Venus, which runs from between the third and fourth fingers to between the first and second fingers; the line of the Sun, which runs from near the wrist to the finger of the Sun; the line of Mars, which runs round the Mount of Venus within the line of Life; the Via Lasciva, which runs parallel to the line of Health further toward the outside of the hand; the line of Intuition, which curves round the Mount of the Moon; and the line of Marriage, which curves across the Mount of Mercury. The Bracelets, which run across the wrist, are taken as indications of the constitution of the subject.

When the palmist has considered the

Below left: a female hand that is both 'psychic' and a typical 'Water' hand, with lunar characteristics. This is a sensitive, changeable person, but the well-developed finger of Jupiter suggests good judgement. The line of Life is strong and well-marked. Although the line of Heart begins quite strongly from below the Mount of Jupiter it breaks before ending, chained, below the Mount of Mercury. It seems as if this person had no one on whom to direct her affection until later life; there is only one 'line of Marriage'. The line of Head begins strongly on the Mount of Jupiter, indicating an ambitious character, but it breaks, revealing inner conflict. The line of Fate begins strongly at the wrist but stops on the line of Heart, perhaps indicating that emotional problems will interfere with her career

Below: hand of a young man before and after psychiatry. The deep line on the Mount of the Moon has almost vanished and the many lines under the finger of Apollo have become one strong line

form of the subject's hand, the relative size of the fingers, and the implications of the various lines, he will turn his attention to the many smaller marks that can be found on the palm surface and on the fingers. He will look particularly for marks in the form of a star, a cross, a square, a circle, a triangle, a tripod or a spearhead. 'Islands' or spots that break up the lines also have their significance.

Palmistry, like astrology and geomancy, is also practised in China; although it is interpreted very differently, the readings obtained nevertheless correlate very closely with those arrived at by Western methods.

Chinese palmistry divides the palm into eight 'Palaces', which are designated by the eight trigrams of the *I Ching* (see page 24). The procedures of Chinese palmistry are thus quite closely related to the initial stages of Western palmistry, in which particular attention is paid to the shape of the hand; considerably less attention is devoted to the significance of the individual lines, which are seen as defining the areas occupied by the eight Palaces.

With this brief description of the techniques of cheiromancy, we come to the end of our consideration of the principal methods of divination practised throughout the world. But there remain perhaps hundreds of minor methods, either peculiar to a particular region, or of such inscrutable complexity that they are understood only by their practitioners.

There are hundreds of textbooks from which the eager enquirer can learn the practice of divination by horoscope, geomancy, the *I Ching*, Tarot cards or palmistry. Those with developed clairvoyant faculties may try 'scrying' with a mirror, a bowl of water or a crystal ball. The businessman who wants advice on his investments, or the general who has hopes of becoming the ruler of his country, no longer expects the diviner to:

Pour in sow's blood that hath eaten
Her nine farrow; grease that sweaten
From the murderer's gibbet throw
Into the flame.

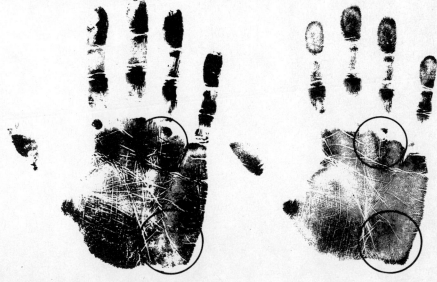

'As above, so below'

Although astrology has always been regarded as a mysterious and occult art, recent research has suggested it is scientifically valid. In the first part of this series, BRIAN INNES asks: what is a horoscope – and is it possible to use it to predict future events?

EVERY DAY, MANY MILLIONS of people turn to a section of the newspaper with a heading such as 'Your Horoscope for Today', and more than 60 per cent believe what they read there. At parties, guests greet one another: 'What are you?' 'I'm a Libran.' 'Oh good, we should get on together, I'm an Aquarian.'

This is the stuff of the common understanding of astrology, and it is arrant nonsense. A horoscope is a map – a rather simple, stylised map – showing the positions of the planets (a term that, in astrology, includes the Sun and Moon) in relation to each other and to Earth; at any given moment, the horoscope is exactly the same for everybody. And to say 'I'm a Libran' is to say no more than 'I was born between 24 September and 23 October'. Yet if you told your fellow guest at a party 'I was born on 10 October', it would sound rather ludicrous for him to reply 'Oh good, I was born on 15 February'; he is far more likely to say 'That means you're a Libran' in a significant tone, as if that implied a lot more.

People who understand astrology, and who take at least some part of it seriously, know that it is a subject far divorced from this popular mumbo-jumbo. They know that it is not a matter of 'What your stars foretell' – and, indeed, the stars themselves do not enter into any astrological calculations. Yet most criticisms by scientists against astrology are directed at just such misunderstandings – the former Astronomer Royal, Dr Harold Spencer Jones, could write, for instance: 'It is significant that I do not know

Above: 'Mars rules in Scorpio by day, and in Aries by night. He exerts his influence in all manly pursuits: fencing and athletics and the arts of war.' An illumination from the 15th-century treatise on astrology, *De sphaera*

Left: the great circular 'calendar stone' that once stood halfway up the pyramid of Tenochtitlan in Mexico. The two circular 'zodiacs' represent all the days of the Mayan year

of any astrologer who is an observer of the stars, nor do I know of any serious observer of the stars who is an astrologer.' It seems, in fact, that most of those who dismiss astrology as pure superstition have never bothered to find out what it is and how it is practised. This dismissive attitude is as intellectually shortsighted as the gullible belief in 'Your Horoscope for Today'.

A science for love and war
Astrology is one of the oldest of the sciences, and for more than 2000 years it was synonymous with astronomy. It was established in Babylonian times, flourished in Egypt, was practised by the Greeks and Romans, and kept alive – like most other sciences – by the Arabs. And as a science it was similarly studied in China, in India, and in central America.

The principle behind the practice of astrology is very pithily expressed in a phrase that was believed to have been coined by

Left: this wooden mummy-case, now in the British Museum, is from west Thebes and once held the body of Sheik Abdu'l-Qurna. It shows the goddess Nut surrounded by signs of the zodiac

Below: how the Sun appears to be in the different constellations of the zodiac. The Earth moves round the Sun, taking 12 months to complete its orbit; and, if it were possible to see the star background to the Sun during daylight, it would appear that the Sun was in a particular constellation throughout each month. It is easy to work out that the constellation due south at midnight is diametrically opposite to the constellation in which the Sun is to be found

the Egyptian magician Hermes Trismegistos ('thrice-great Hermes'): 'As above, so below.' In other words, events on Earth reflect those in the heavens. The astrologers saw the planets – the word means 'wanderers' in Greek – moving purposefully or erratically against the background of the starry skies; and they supposed that the actions and experiences of these distant gods would be reflected in human affairs. When Mars, the god of war, burnt angrily in the night sky it was a time for quarrels and martial pursuits; when Venus glowed brightly as night fell, it was a time for love.

Circle of animals

The astrologers soon observed that the planets stayed within quite a narrow band of the sky, never moving far away from the path of the Sun – the ecliptic. This band was marked by particular constellations and, since there were 12 months (moon cycles) in the year that it took the Sun to return to its original position, they identified 12 constellations as marking the months. At some time very early in the history of astrology in Babylonia, these constellations were given the names of mythic animals or persons, and the word zodiac means 'circle of animals' in Greek.

In fact, the 12 constellations do not divide the year equally between them, and few of them even vaguely resemble the animal they are named for. Worse than that: when we say (for instance) that Mars is in Aries – that is, apparently making a statement that Mars in the night sky can be seen against a background of the constellation Aries – this is just not true. Some 3000 to 4000 years ago, however, it was true.

As we now know, the Sun and the other planets do not move round the Earth; it is the Earth that moves, like the other planets,

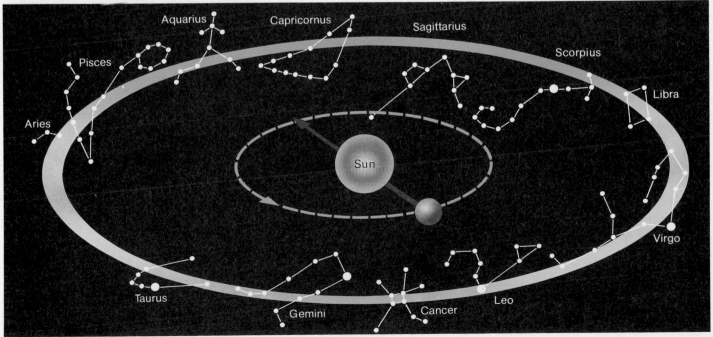

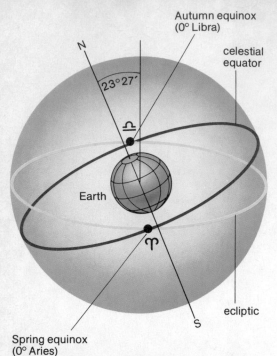

Autumn equinox
(0° Libra)

celestial
equator

23°27′

♎

Earth

♈

ecliptic

N

S

Spring equinox
(0° Aries)

Left: in all simple astronomical and navigational calculations, the Earth is envisaged at the centre of the celestial sphere, which revolves along the line of the Earth's equator, while the apparent path of the Sun, the ecliptic, is at an angle to it. The equinoxes are the two points at which the ecliptic intersects with the celestial equator, and are defined as 0° Aries in spring, and 0° Libra in autumn

equally divided between night and day; these are the spring and autumn equinoxes, which occur usually on 20 or 21 March, and 22 or 23 September.

Four thousand years ago, when astrology was young, the Sun was in the constellation of Aries – or, more accurately, that twelfth of the zodiac in which Aries is situated – at the spring equinox. About 2000 years ago, the point on the zodiac circle marking the Sun's 'entering' at the spring equinox was therefore designated 0° Aries, the autumn equinox being 0° Libra.

Night and day

But the Earth is not just leaning to one side as it circles the Sun; it is also wobbling very slowly like a spinning top that is beginning to slow down. As a result, the direction in which it leans gradually changes. This gives rise to a phenomenon known as the 'precession of the equinoxes', which was discovered by the Greek astronomer Hipparchus about 120 BC; the result of the wobbling is that the position of the spring equinox constantly moves: in

round the Sun, so that the Sun is against a different part of the background zodiac every day, and against a different constellation every month. In fact, of course, the Sun is so bright by day that we cannot see its star background; but during the night we can see the parts of the zodiac that are opposite the Sun by 12 hours, and so easily work out which constellation the Sun is 'in'.

However, the Earth, as it goes round the Sun, leans its axis of rotation by 23°27′ to the side. When the northern pole is leaning toward the Sun it is summer in the northern hemisphere, and the days are long; in winter the northern pole is leaning away from the Sun, and days are short. There are only two days every year on which the 24 hours are

Right: a diagram of the phenomenon known as the precession of the equinoxes. The spring and autumn equinoxes are those two days in the year when day and night are of equal length; and because the Earth is slowly wobbling on its axis, the Sun appears in a different place in the zodiac each year at the equinox. About 4000 years ago the Sun was moving into Aries at the spring equinox (top); it gradually appeared to move backward through Aries, so that after about 2000 years it was at 0° Aries, and about to move into Pisces (middle). The position of the Sun at the spring equinox was then named 0° Aries, and this has defined the zodiac circle ever since. The equinox has now moved most of the way through Pisces, and within some 20 years will 'enter' Aquarius (bottom) – but the spring equinox will still be 0° Aries

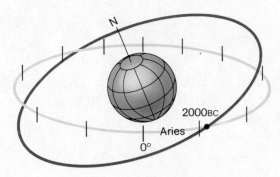

N

2000 BC

Aries

0°

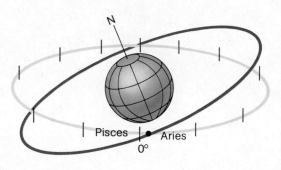

N

Pisces

Aries

0°

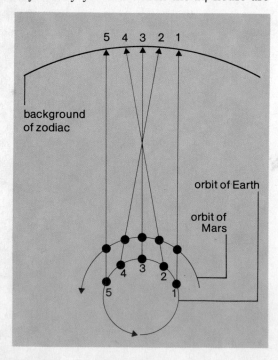

5 4 3 2 1

background
of zodiac

orbit of Earth

orbit of
Mars

4 3 2
5 1

Left: the word planet means 'wanderer', and many of the planets appear to move erratically about the sky, sometimes apparently going back on their tracks for days or weeks. In the diagram, it is clear how Mars appears to move backward between positions 2 and 4

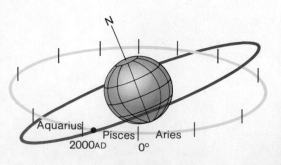

N

Aquarius

Pisces

Aries

2000 AD

0°

2000 years it moved right through 30° of Aries, and it is now most of the way through Pisces. As we near the end of the 20th century, the spring equinox is moving out of Pisces and into Aquarius. This is what is meant by 'the dawning of the Age of Aquarius'. In another 20,000 years the equinox will once more be at 0°Aries. But, for navigational, astronomical and astrological purposes, the spring equinox is always designated 0°Aries.

This, then, is one of the reasons why popular talk about 'sun signs' has so little significance. Three thousand years ago, when we said of somebody's birth that the Sun was in Scorpio, we meant just that; 1000 years ago it was in Libra; soon it will be in Virgo. But we still say of someone born in November that they are a Scorpian.

It is, in fact, the movements of the planets themselves that we are concerned with, not the star background against which they can be seen. They are like the many hands of a giant astronomical clock, and in recording their exact positions we are identifying a precise moment. This is what the horoscope does: it pinpoints the positions of the planets in the zodiac, as seen from Earth, and also their positions in relation to one another.

To the ancient astrologers the argument was transparently obvious. Since events in heaven were reflected by events on Earth, and since it was possible to predict the future positions of the gods (the planets) months or years in advance, then from knowledge of those positions it should be easy to predict events upon Earth.

Planets are not gods . . .
Modern critics of astrology, who know that the planets are not gods and that heavenly phenomena are not reflected in earthly happenings, find it easy to dismiss the whole matter. There is no way in which some remote pieces of rock (or balls of gas) can affect human nature and destiny, they claim. And they are perhaps right.

However, this argument does not rule out the possibility of prediction. Suppose you

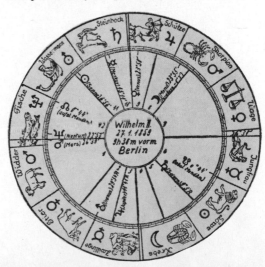

Above: 'May', from the 15th-century codex *Les très riches heures du Duc de Berry*. The month, as the portion of the zodiac above the illustration shows, is divided between Taurus and Gemini

Left: a conventional horoscope drawn for Kaiser Wilhelm II. The horoscope is divided into 12 'houses' that do not correspond with the 12 signs of the zodiac; while the positions of the planets are indicated as degrees of angle within each zodiac division

receive a letter from your uncle, saying that he will be leaving his country home at about 10.15 a.m. and asking you to meet his train. A glance at the timetable will tell you that the only train he could possibly catch will arrive at the terminus at 1.05 p.m. An enquiry at the station will tell you that the train normally arrives at platform three. If you have a contact in the railway offices, you can probably discover the name of the driver of the train, the colour of the engine and its head code, and possibly all sorts of related facts.

If you take a friend with you to the station, you can tell him a surprising amount about future events. Pointing to the station clock, you tell him that when the two hands are together – in astrological terms this would be described as 'in conjunction' – a number of things will happen: a blue engine (and you may even know its name and number), with the head code o6 and driven by a man named Harry Grimshaw, will arrive at platform three, and that a middle-aged man with glasses, walking with a stick, will get down from it. Your friend will be amazed: how could all these events have been caused by the influence of two hands on a clock?

The astrologer works with something very like a railway timetable. It is called an *ephemeris*, and it gives the positions of the various planets in the heavens at any particular time. Astronomers use very similar tables, and so do all sea and air navigators – in fact it is possible to draw up a horoscope perfectly satisfactorily from a 'nautical almanac'.

Astronomical aspects

It has been objected that the discovery of the planets Uranus, Neptune, and Pluto, which were unknown to the ancient astrologers, must have invalidated everything that went before. However these distant planets are relatively slow-moving, like hands on a clock that tell the century, the decade and the year. Uranus, for instance, remained in Libra from 1968 until December 1974; Neptune entered Sagittarius in 1970 and leaves it in 1984; Pluto takes from 1971 to 1983 to pass through Libra. So the 'influence' of these planets in the horoscope is equally slow-moving; of far greater significance to the modern astrologer is the relation of the position of one planet to another, something which is called its 'aspect'.

Astrological interpretation, in fact, falls into two distinct parts. First comes the drawing up of a horoscope. This need not be drawn up for the moment of a person's birth; it can just as well be for an event like a wedding or the issue of some new company stock. However, the Moon and Mercury move very rapidly through the horoscope, resulting in quickly changing aspects, and so the moment for which the horoscope is drawn should be defined as accurately as possible. It is mainly for this reason that the

horoscopes most commonly drawn are natal horoscopes.

From a natal horoscope an astrologer claims to be able to make a detailed description of the physical attributes and spiritual nature of its subject, based upon 4000 years of experience. Working from such a deep understanding of the subject, it is then possible to make predictions of the way in which he or she will behave and develop in the future. Few present-day astrologers, even the most famous and successful, go much beyond this point. They may suggest, after calculating the future positions of the planets, the most favourable time for some enterprise, but not many are prepared to make detailed predictions of future events.

The truly predictive part of astrology, in fact, is a complex and time-consuming operation. It is necessary to draw up the horoscopes for various precisely defined times in the future, and then to relate these to the natal horoscope of the person whose fate is being considered. It is here that astrology

Right: a set of horoscopes cast by the English astrologer (but drawn up after the event) for the birth, coronation and death of Louis XVI of France and his queen Marie-Antoinette

begins to lose its credibility, for astrologers – in order to cut down the time involved in going through a succession of constantly changing horoscopes – have introduced the concept of 'secondary directions'. By this means the subject's horoscope is 'progressed' by periods of a day from the moment of birth, each day's changes in the positions of the planets being taken to represent a year, or a month, or a week in the subject's life – whichever the astrologer prefers. Whatever justification there may be for believing that the accurately drawn horoscope does contain useful information, there is none whatsoever for this artificial principle of progression.

Left: a horoscope for the birth of John Milton, drawn up by the English astrologer John Gadbury. It is drawn in typical 17th-century style – the 12 triangular divisions surrounding the central square each represent one of the 12 'houses'

Millions of people scan their 'stars' in the newspapers every day. But a horoscope prepared for an individual would read very differently. This chapter explains how such a detailed chart of the heavens is drawn up

A HOROSCOPE IS A MAP – a map of the zodiac circle, with the Earth at its centre, and all the planets in the positions in which they can be seen from Earth. Some of the planets move relatively fast – the Moon, for instance, moves through more than one third of one 'sign' of the zodiac in the course of 24 hours – so the appearance of this map changes from minute to minute.

The basis of the horoscope has changed very little in 5000 years. The ancient Babylonians recognised that the stars were on a sphere that revolved once about the Earth

An illustration from the 17th-century atlas *Harmonia macrocosmica* by Andreas Cellarius. Viewed from the southern hemisphere, the constellations of the zodiac run in reverse order, from Taurus, here seen as the ascendant sign, through Aries, Pisces, Aquarius and Capricorn, to Sagittarius disappearing below the western horizon

every day, but that shifted very slightly in each revolution so that it did not return to its original orientation until the year had passed. Within this sphere the planets circled the Earth: the Sun went round the Earth once a day, the Moon rather faster, so that it passed through all the constellations of the zodiac in the time it took the Sun to pass through one. The other planets moved at different speeds, sometimes moving fast in one direction, then hesitating and going back on their tracks before moving forward again. This picture of the Universe is still employed in all navigational calculations and in many everyday astronomical ones.

Of course, we cannot see the stars in the daytime, nor can we see what is below the Earth's rim at night, but it does not require much observation to be able to work out that

How to cast a horoscope

the stars remain fixed in their positions on the heavenly sphere, so we know exactly where they are in relation to the Earth, even when they cannot be seen.

Stand facing due south on a clear night at about midnight. To make things easily understandable, the winter solstice, just before the end of December, is a good time to choose for this example; and, for convenience, assume you are in the northern hemisphere. At that time of year the Sun is said to be moving from Sagittarius into Capricorn but, because of the precession of the equinoxes, it is actually in Scorpio. Since it is

midnight, the constellation of Scorpius will be directly beneath your feet, and the constellation of Taurus will be visible in the southern sky. Eastward from Taurus, the constellations will be Gemini, Cancer, and Leo; westward they will be Aries and Pisces.

That is what you will actually see in the sky; but all astronomical and navigational tables are based on the assumption that the spring equinox is still at 0° Aries, as it was nearly 2000 years ago. So we must now imagine an entirely artificial zodiac circle, in which the Sun is just entering Capricorn, with Cancer just coming to the mid-heaven in the southern sky at midnight; then, eastward, the zodiac signs will be Leo and Virgo, with Libra just appearing over the eastern horizon; and westward will be Gemini and Taurus, with Aries disappearing below the western horizon.

The zodiac in the heavens
We begin to draw our horoscope, therefore, as a circle, divided into 12 equal parts to represent the 12 parts of the zodiac, which approximate to the 12 months. The top of the circle represents the mid-heaven, the highest point of the Sun's daily travel, and to the left and right are the eastern and western horizons. As the Earth revolves (from right to left, as it were), Libra will gradually rise in the east; at midnight of the winter solstice it is the ascendant sign. At dawn the ascendant sign will be Capricorn; and at midday the

ascendant sign will be Aries.

At midnight, the Sun will be in the lowest part of our circular map, and so we mark it there. On the night of 22 December 1980, it was at 1° Capricorn. Mercury and Venus always remain fairly close to the Sun, and so they will not be visible in the midnight sky. In fact, on the night we have chosen, only the Moon is visible, almost due south and high in the sky; Mars, Jupiter and Saturn are below the horizon. From a set of tables known as an *ephemeris* we can get the figures for their positions: Mercury at 26° Sagittarius, Venus at 6° Sagittarius, Mars at 23° Capricorn, Jupiter at 9° Libra, Saturn at 9° Libra (in what is called a conjunction between Jupiter and Saturn).

There are also, of course, the planets that we cannot see, and that were only discovered within the last 200 years. Uranus is at 28° Scorpio, Neptune at 23° Sagittarius, and Pluto at 24° Libra. We can see from these figures that later in the night, before sunrise, first Jupiter and Saturn will rise, then (if we could only see it) Pluto, then Uranus, then Venus, Neptune and Mercury (the morning star) in that order. Mars will not be visible because the Sun will rise before it, and once the Sun has risen the stars and planets cannot be seen.

To draw up an accurate horoscope, so as to get the ascendant and the mid-heaven in exactly the right orientation, clock time is not

Left: this third-century Roman mosaic shows the close relationship between Ea, the Babylonian god of the oceans, and Poseidon, the Greek and Roman god. As *suhumarshu*, the fish-goat, Ea gave his name to the constellation we now call Capricorn

Below: the sky as it appeared in the northern hemisphere at midnight on 22 December 1980, together with the portion of sky containing the other half of the ecliptic that cannot be seen at night (bottom), and the equivalent horoscope for that hour (below right). In the sky, Taurus is in mid-heaven, and the Sun is 'in' the constellation Scorpius. In the horoscope, which makes no allowance for the precession of the equinoxes, the Sun is in Capricorn

Far right: in traditional astrology, each sign of the zodiac is associated with a particular part of the body

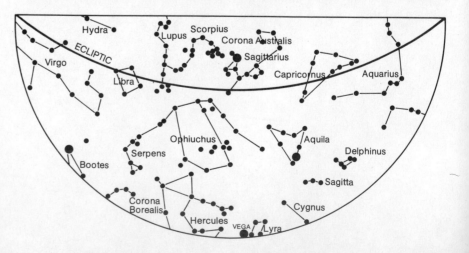

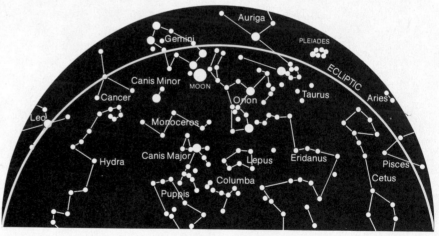

♑	Capricorn
♒	Aquarius
♓	Pisces
♈	Aries
♉	Taurus
♊	Gemini
♋	Cancer
♌	Leo
♍	Virgo
♎	Libra
♏	Scorpio
♐	Sagittarius
☉	Sun
☽	Moon
☿	Mercury
♀	Venus
⊕	Earth
♂	Mars
♃	Jupiter
♄	Saturn
♅	Uranus
♆	Neptune
♇	Pluto

sufficiently accurate. Clock time is derived from Greenwich Mean Time; that is, from a calculation of the average length of a day, and the establishment of the average time at which the Sun is due south and at its zenith – because of small variations in the movement of the Earth, midday by Sun time can be as much as 20 minutes out. Astrologers therefore use star time, or 'sidereal time', which is similarly measured from the equinox; astronomers also use sidereal time to calculate at which part of the sky to point their telescopes, so that they can observe a particular star at a particular time.

Casting a horoscope

It is also necessary to make corrections for local clock time. When it is midnight in Britain, on or near the Greenwich meridian, it is midday in the central Pacific, with the Sun blazing high in the sky, and the sign of Aries just rising on the eastern horizon. Fortunately the calculations to change local time to GMT and then to sidereal time are very simple; once they are done it is a matter of minutes to look up the planetary positions in the *ephemeris* and draw up the horoscope.

This, then, is a horoscope: a map showing the positions of the planets relative to one another, and their orientation within the zodiac circle. Earth is the small dot at the centre of the circle, and all the way down the Greenwich meridian to the equator the horoscope remains essentially the same. Below the equator, where the Sun appears not in the southern sky but the northern sky, the map,

or horoscope, is simply inverted.

The interpretation of the horoscope is based upon certain long-established rules. The Sun represents the real self, the fundamental ego; the ascendant represents the physical characteristics, the outward appearance; and the Moon denotes the soul, the subconscious psychological nature. In the horoscope we have drawn up the Sun is unequivocally in Capricorn, and will remain there for nearly four weeks; the Moon is in Cancer for two days before moving into Leo; and the ascendant sign is Libra.

In popular magazine astrology, it is only the position of the Sun that is considered: someone born in late December or the first three weeks of January is a Capricornian, and

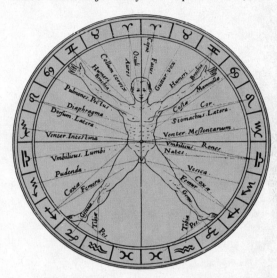

that is all that need be said. Capricornians, say the astrological textbooks, are strong-willed but self-centred, suspicious of others, clever in argument but likely to lose control of the situation by a sudden outbreak of irresponsibility. But Moon in Cancer denotes someone who is emotionally committed to domestic security and a stable marriage; while the ascendant Libra suggests someone of average height, well-formed and good-looking, with long blond hair, blue eyes and a healthy complexion.

Conjunctions and characters

This is just the beginning of astrological interpretation. Venus in Sagittarius is supposed to indicate a frank and open person, but one who values religious conformity; while Mercury and Neptune in conjunction in Sagittarius would be interpreted as revealing someone who could gain a reputation as a prophet. Mars in Capricorn denotes the attainment of material success and social standing; Jupiter and Saturn conjunct in Libra suggest someone who will apply experience to the settling of all kinds of problems, and probably become wealthy thereby.

There is no doubt that this kind of analysis already begins to give us a picture of a certain kind of person; whether any of those born at midnight on 22 December 1980 really

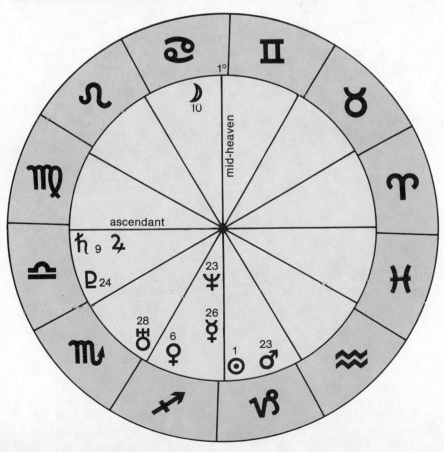

Right: in India, as in all other developed cultures of the world, astrology was long established as a science. This border design, from the early 17th-century *Jahangir's album*, reveals that the working tools of the astrologer have hardly changed in the course of many hundreds of years

develop in this way remains to be seen. Traditional astrology goes further; and it is particularly in these further refinements that modern scientific research has shown some correlation with the traditional beliefs.

Planetary aspects

In the more detailed analysis, the 'aspects' become of particular importance. These are the positions of the planets relative to one another in the sky. We all know, for instance, that when the Sun and Moon are in conjunction, or when they are opposed, as in the horoscope under discussion, the aggregate gravitational pull produces the phenomenon known as spring tides; while when the two are at right angles to one another – square, as it is known in astrology – the height of tides is at a minimum and we get neap tides. A similar kind of gravitational effect can be envisaged as being produced by the smaller or more distant planets: two planets conjunct or opposed reinforce each other's effect; two planets square to one another – separated by 90° or three zodiac signs – reduce each other's effect; and planets 'trine' to one another – that is, making up the points of an equilateral triangle, and separated one from the other by 120° or four signs of the zodiac – are balanced when there are planets at all three points of the triangle, but otherwise 'drag', as it were, the planetary effect to one side when there are only two.

One other element of astrological interpretation needs to be considered before the significance of the horoscope is fully understood. The ancient Babylonians saw the planets wandering about the sky like travellers in the desert; and they imagined that

Right: an Arabic model of the celestial sphere, made in the 18th century

Far right: a diagrammatic representation of the celestial sphere. The stars should be imagined painted on the inside surface of the sphere, with the Earth as a tiny point at the centre. The thick horizontal ring represents the horizon, so that the part of the heavens visible at any time is the interior surface of the sphere above the horizon. The celestial equator is the projection of the Earth's equator onto the sphere, and the ecliptic represents the apparent path of the Sun. The zodiac constellations lie in a band along the ecliptic. The sphere is envisaged divided into 12 'houses', each house being the home of one of the planets

every so often they returned to their own houses, which they ruled like the master or mistress of a household. The Sun, obviously, was at the height of his powers in midsummer: he ruled in the house of Leo. The Moon, the queen of the planets, sat at the Sun's left hand: she ruled in Cancer. The other five planets, who roamed through day and night, each had two houses: one for daytime, and one for night-time. Thus Mercury ruled in the day house of Virgo, and in the night house of Gemini; Saturn ruled in Capricorn as his day house, and in Aquarius at night; and so on. When the planets were in their houses, their influence was believed to be particularly strong.

A rather different concept of houses was subsequently introduced: in due course some

astrologers began to define the mid-heaven as the dividing line between two houses. If this is so, and we then divide the horoscope into 12 houses of equal size, that to the east of the zenith will contain 29° of the sign at the zenith and 1° of the next sign west, and so on all round the circle. The great astronomer and astrologer Ptolemy, who practised in Alexandria in the second century AD, employed this method of house division, which is known as the 'equal house' method.

Arabian wisdom

In later centuries the Arabs, who had gained possession of all the ancient manuscripts from the library at Alexandria, became fascinated with mathematics, and introduced all sorts of complicated methods of calculating house divisions. The equal house system of Ptolemy divides the ecliptic – the apparent path of the Sun through the zodiac – into 12 equal houses. The system of the Arab mathematician Ibn Ezra – known in Europe as the Regiomontanus system – divides the celestial equator into 12 equal houses. This is all very well for astrologers near the Earth's equator, for there the difference is negligible, but in the high latitudes as much as 50° of the zodiac must be crammed within 30° of the horoscope for certain signs, while other signs must be stretched so that only 15° occupy one twelfth of the horoscope. There are other systems, based on different principles, but the most ridiculous of all is the system of Placidus. This is based upon the *time* taken by any degree of the zodiac to rise from the lowest part of the horoscope circle to the mid-heaven. Since above the Arctic Circle many degrees of the zodiac remain always above the horizon, these parts of the zodiac do not appear in a Placidean horoscope at all. The only reason why this extraordinary system has survived is that the most readily available *ephemeris* is Raphael's, which contains tables of houses according to Placidus.

Each house of the horoscope is also credited with controlling some part of the

Above: another illustration from the 15th-century manuscript *De sphaera*. The Sun rules only by day, and his house is in Leo. The human occupations over which he exerts a particularly strong influence are concerned with power and domination over other people

subject's destiny, from servants, conditions of employment, illness and recovery (house 6) to secrecy, the psychic faculties and places of concealment (house 12); but astrologers have never been able to agree on whether the division of the horoscope into 12 equal houses should be made from the ascendant, or the mid-heaven, or whether the ascendant or the mid-heaven should fall in the middle of its respective house. Houses are considered very important by many modern astrologers – they are held to represent, in a unique way, the fate of the individual. But the confusion about house division means the significance of the various planets relative to their houses has always been a little obscure.

This has been a very brief survey of the beliefs involved in the interpretation of a drawn-up horoscope; but some understanding of the principles involved is necessary in order to appreciate the remarkable discoveries that have been made in the past decade, discoveries that suggest there may be some justification in the age-old beliefs of astrology.

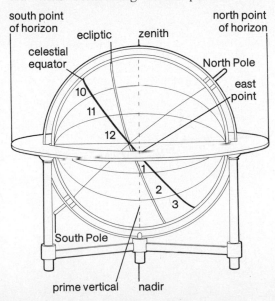

south point of horizon
north point of horizon
ecliptic
zenith
celestial equator
North Pole
10
east point
11
12
1
2
3
South Pole
prime vertical
nadir

ASTROLOGY IS A VERY ANCIENT SCIENCE: its tenets and principles have come down to us over thousands of years, so that now it is impossible to separate the original beliefs from those that have accrued to them over so many generations. Yet much of what is today considered traditional in astrology comes from no farther back than the end of the 19th century – a time when the study of astrology was suddenly revived in both England and France. The association of astrology with the Tarot cards, for instance, dates from this period; there is no historical connection whatsoever between the two, except insofar as the 22 Tarot trumps are the remnants of a much larger set of some 50 cards that at one time included 12 that represented the signs of the zodiac, with another seven to represent the planets.

Some measure of the confusion created by the 19th-century occultists can be obtained from the so-called 'tables of correspondences' published in 1909 in *Liber 777* by Aleister Crowley. There are altogether 194 tables, which provide the equivalents of the letters of the Hebrew alphabet to the planets, the spheres and the elements; to colours, Tarot cards, Egyptian, Roman and Hindu gods and goddesses, plants, precious stones, drugs, perfumes, and all sorts of concepts.

Magic and number symbolism

Crowley made much of this up for himself; parts he got from English occultists of the 1880s and 1890s such as L. Macgregor Mathers; some can be traced back to medieval magical writers such as Cornelius Agrippa; and a few scraps can be attributed to Roman astrology and to the beliefs associated with the Jewish *qabalah*. This system of 'correspondences' is very clearly a development of the 'as above, so below' principle designed to cover every contingency. Although it is completely artificial, this sort of thing is frequently made an essential part of what is taught in contemporary courses in astrology.

The sceptic may be forgiven for finding some of the fundamental principles of astrology equally questionable. When one reads, for instance, that the typical Pisces native has unusually prominent eyes and a fleshy body, with some kind of peculiarity about the feet, and that he or she is likely to be a good swimmer, one is justified in suspecting that the description is tailored to result in something that is essentially fish-like. This apparent anthropomorphism turns up throughout astrology: the Cancerian, for example is said to walk with a peculiar sideways gait; the Sagittarian has a long face with prominent front teeth, and female Sagittarians may wear their hair in a pony-tail; the Taurean is obstinate, with a broad face and thick-set body, and a thick muscular throat.

The characters supposed to be exhibited by the different planets seem to suffer from

Astrologers have always held that the planets influence our lives in quite specific ways. This chapter describes how – and reviews some modern research that may back up the astrologers' claims

A giant solar flare, perhaps as much as 100,000 miles in length. The Sun plays such a major part in the lives of everyone on Earth that it is hard to believe that it has no effect upon the destiny of those born at different stages of its annual cycle. The observations made by John Nelson suggest that the relative positions of the planets affect activities on the surface of the Sun and, therefore, the amount of cosmic radiation falling upon the Earth

the same kind of identification. Waite's *Compendium of natal astrology* lists the following 'personal characteristics shown by the planets':

Sun: pride, generosity, egotism, honour, loyalty, ardour, vitality

Moon: sensitivity, sentiment, maternal instinct, femininity, changeableness

Mercury: quickness, sharpness, braininess, ready wit, flow of words

Venus: beauty, grace, charm, artistic tastes, affection, sociability

Mars: virility, energy, courage, initiative, impulsiveness, passion, aggression

Jupiter: optimism, cheer, generosity, joviality, sport, strength, nobility, ceremoniousness

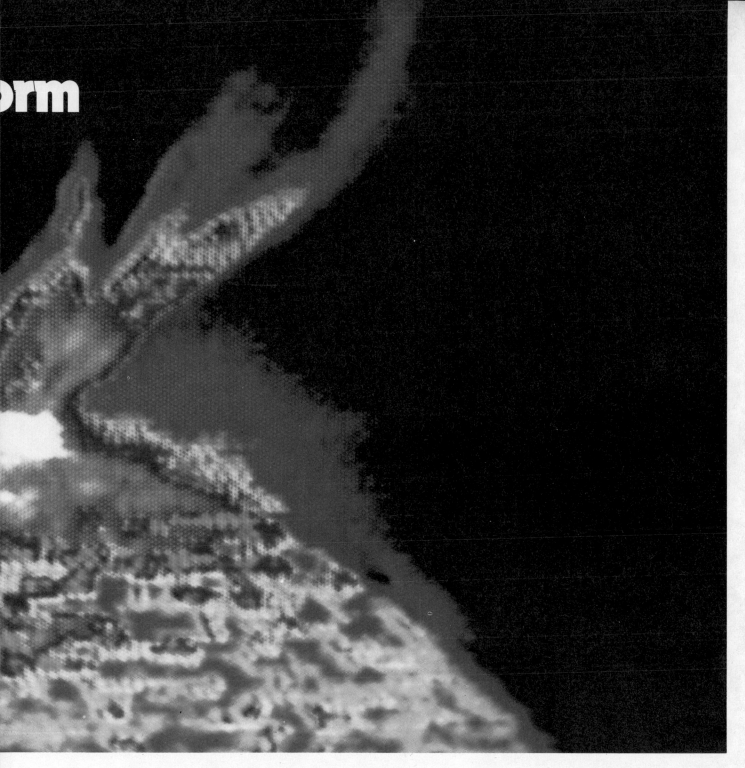

Saturn: caution, taciturnity, pessimism, self-restraint, profundity, steadfastness

(There are also characteristics given for Uranus, Neptune and Pluto, but they are less important and need not concern us here.)

These are, of course, the characteristics that one would expect the various gods to possess – but why has any particular god's name been given to any particular planet? Mars, of course, by its red coloration, can be identified with the god of war and so with what are generally considered essentially masculine traits; but why should one small, bright, quickly moving planet be identified with ready wit and braininess, while the other is identified with beauty and charm; why should one distant and slow-moving body represent optimism and generosity, while another represents caution and pessimism?

It is when we come to look at the Sun that a possible explanation begins to emerge. Nobody would object to a statement of the following general kind: that children born at midday in high summer tend to be very different in personality from those born at midnight in winter. Many people who would not subscribe to any of astrology's beliefs remain convinced that the season, the time of day and the weather prevailing at the moment a child is born can affect its nature and the way in which it will behave.

Following this line of argument, it is not

difficult to develop the statement above. Consider the following:

Recent investigations by a well-known market research bureau have revealed that a high proportion of children born at or near midday during the first two weeks of August are healthier than the national average, generally strong and tall, and frequently blond. As they develop they show good qualities of leadership, being both practical and kind-hearted.

True or not, this is a plausible statement, and would be given due consideration by even the most sceptical scientists; however, had it begun 'Leos tend to be . . .' it would be likely to evoke cries of 'Nonsense!' and 'Superstition!' from the most broad-minded of astronomers and other members of the scientific establishment, so nervous are they of the subject of astrology.

And yet, as has already been pointed out, to say that the Sun is in Leo is to say no more than that the date is somewhere between 22 July and 21 August. Could it be, in fact, that the part of the zodiac in which the Sun is found at this time of year has been named Leo *because* the experience of centuries showed that those born in what we call August tended to exhibit leonine characteristics? After all, the shape of the constellation itself bears little if any resemblance to a lion – and indeed, the precession of the equinoxes means that during August the Sun is now really in Cancer.

It is possible, then, that all the constellations of the zodiac have been named for the characteristics exhibited by those born at that particular time of year. We are dealing with a mass of information gathered over nearly 2000 years by the astrologers of Babylon and their successors – far more detailed than the statistics assembled by the mythical market research bureau invoked above. And it is possible that the names of the planets equally indicate the temperaments of

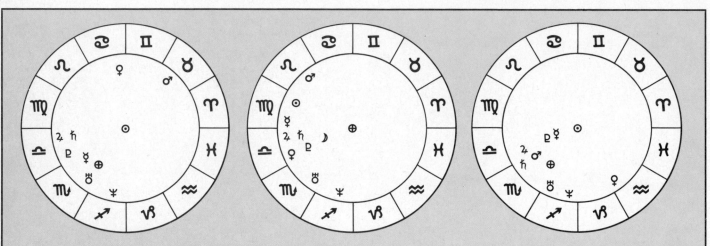

The Jupiter effect

Much has been made of the so-called 'Jupiter effect'. Jupiter and Saturn, the two largest planets, come into conjunction, or within a degree or two of one another, every 20 years or so. Such an event occurred in 1980–1981. Seen from the Earth, Saturn and Jupiter were in conjunction from November 1980 to March 1981, and again in August; seen from the Sun, they were in conjunction in May 1981. In 1974, in the first edition of their book *The Jupiter effect*, John Gribbin and S. Plagemann suggested that this conjunction would be accompanied by the lining up of most of the other planets – and Arthur Prieditis, an American writer, predicted 'world-shattering upheavals of the first magnitude'.

As seen from the Earth, the nearest to a lining up of planets occurred in early September 1981, when Saturn and Jupiter were respectively in 12° and 9° Libra, Pluto was in 22°, and Venus

Jupiter and Saturn were in conjunction relative to the Sun in May 1981 (left); all planets were together on one side of the Earth in September 1981 (centre); and the closest grouping relative to the Sun occurred in May 1982 (right).
Below: John Gribbin

passed through Libra in the course of about three weeks, while the Moon was in Libra from 31 August to 2 September. The Sun did not enter Libra until nearly the end of the month. Throughout this month, Mercury was in Virgo and Mars in Leo, while Uranus was in Scorpio and Neptune in Sagittarius.

We now know, of course, that the cataclysmic events described by Prieditis failed to happen. Gribbin, indeed, withdrew much of the substance of his forecast before the dates concerned.

The closest grouping of planets relative to the Sun occurred about 20 May, when Saturn, Jupiter, Pluto, Mars and Mercury were all within about 17°; at this time the Earth was in mid Scorpio, Venus in Aquarius, Uranus and Neptune in Sagittarius. But again, we now know that nothing of momentous significance happened in May – nothing, for example, to compare with the British victory in the Falkland Islands or the Israeli invasion of the Lebanon, both of which occurred in *June* 1982.

those born when the particular planet was dominant in the horoscope.

As we have seen, the horoscope is a time-map of a particular moment. For a person born at that moment, it gives their 'Sun-sign' – it tells us in which twelfth of the year the birth takes place; it gives us the time of day, in terms both of the position of the Sun in the horoscope circle and of the sign ascendant on the eastern horizon; and it also provides us with the relative positions in the heavens of up to nine other 'markers'.

The most important of these is the Moon, which moves right through each of the signs of the zodiac in less than three days. We accept that Sun and Moon exert a very great influence upon human lives: the Sun because it provides light and heat, and is essential for the production of food and the two together because they combine or oppose their gravitational forces to produce the tides. This is not the place to pursue the argument that mankind has evolved from an essentially aquatic animal, and that there is no reason to suppose that we do not remain as sensitive to tidal forces as present-day fish and plankton. Let us accept it as a possibility, and consider the way in which the movement of the planets can affect the nature of the gravitational and magnetic fields within the solar system.

The solar connection

In the mid 1940s, an engineer with RCA Communications Inc. named John Nelson set up a telescope on the roof of the company's office building in central Manhattan, and began to study the Sun. Nelson knew that unusual sunspot activity was accompanied by serious interruption of radio communications, and his job was to find some way of predicting the occurrence of these 'cosmic storms'. He knew little of astronomy and nothing of astrology, but in due course he discovered that there was a direct connection between intense solar disturbance and the relative positions of the planets – their astrological aspects.

By 1967, Nelson could claim a success rate of 93 per cent in his predictions of severe cosmic storms, out of a total of 1460 specific forecasts. For a severe storm, one of the four inner planets (Mercury, Venus, Earth or Mars) must be at an angle of 0°, 90° or 180° with another planet further from the Sun – relative to the Sun as centre. In addition, at least two other planets must be in an 'angular harmonic' relationship with the first pair, the principal harmonics employed by Nelson being the subdivisions by 2, 3, 4, 5 or 6 of 360° – that is, 180°, 120°, 90°, 72° and 60°. Could it possibly be that it is no more than a happy coincidence that Mercury – traditionally associated with communication by all astrologers – appeared to be the most significant planet in Nelson's investigations?

As Guy Lyon Playfair and Scott Hill put it in their book *The cycles of heaven*, 'Nelson's

Right: Jupiter, from *De sphaera*. He signifies physical well-being and material success

Below: three of John Nelson's charts, showing planetary positions relative to the Sun when severe magnetic storms took place. Between 23 and 27 March 1940 (top), seven planets were either square or in opposition. From 12 to 16 November 1960 (centre) occurred the worst storm in 20 years, as predicted by Nelson. The greatest ever recorded cosmic shower was on 23 February 1956 (bottom)

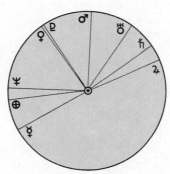

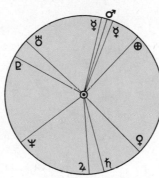

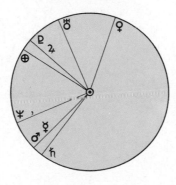

work is an example of what astrology may once have been and still could be: the study of the celestial motions and the *correct* interpretation of their terrestrial effects.' The nature of these terrestrial effects is so far undetermined; it may be no more than some kind of gravitational tide, or it may be the flood of cosmic radiation that accompanies a solar eruption. Many biologists certainly believe that violent cosmic storms can have the most marked effects upon evolution, and meteorologists understand only too well their effect upon the weather. As for the cause of the solar eruptions, it is hardly far-fetched to suggest that they could be the outcome of some kind of solar tidal surge due to the positions of the planets in relation to the Sun.

There are, then, at least two lines of enquiry to be followed. First: since Nelson's work has established a close connection between the positions of the planets relative to the Sun and the outbreak of unusual sunspot activity, is it possible to establish any similar kind of relationship between the aspects of the planets to the Earth and the birth of babies with particular kinds of personality? Second: if this kind of relationship could be proved – which would amount virtually to a proof of some of the most fundamental beliefs of astrology – was the influence upon the development of personality due to gravitational effects, or to the occurrence of different intensities of cosmic shower?

Not long after Nelson had erected his telescope on the roof of the RCA building, and well before the results of his research became public, a young French statistician named Michel Gauquelin, with a sceptical interest in astrology, set out to answer the first question – with unexpected results.

In the past 20 years, researchers have produced some startling evidence that appears to back up traditional astrological beliefs. This chapter investigates their findings

WHEN THE YOUNG FRENCH STATISTICIAN Michel Gauquelin began his investigations in 1950, it was his intention to prove that there was no connection between planetary positions at a person's birth and his future development. He had some previous examples before him: a rather superficial investigation by the famous psychologist C. G. Jung into the astrological relationships of married couples, which he had abandoned as the results became progressively more inconclusive, a vast accumulation of data by K. E. Krafft, the Swiss who was rumoured to have been Hitler's private astrologer, and a statistical analysis by the French astrologer Paul Choisnard, who claimed significant results in such relationships as Sun-Mars in cases of premature death, Mercury-Moon in the nativities of philosophers, Sun-Moon in those of celebrities, and the aspects of Mars in the birth charts of soldiers.

Gauquelin began by comparing the horoscopes of some 25,000 subjects; in France and other countries where it is legally required to register the time of birth of a child, it is possible to calculate accurate horoscopes from birth certificates without the necessity of approaching the individuals concerned. He was soon able to state with confidence that there were no grounds for the wild claims made by Krafft and Choisnard. There

The signs of success

was, however, a lesser piece of research carried out by another French astrologer, Leon Lasson, who had found a significant correlation between Mars and its aspects with the ascendants or descendants of 134 politicians, between Venus and its aspects with the ascendants of 190 artists, and between Mercury and the ascendants or descendants of 209 actors and writers.

Putting his data to this test, Gauquelin was surprised to discover that he obtained the same kind of correlation. Taking a sample of no less than 576 eminent professors of medicine, he found that an unexpectedly high proportion were born just after Mars or Saturn had risen or passed the midheaven. In a second group of 508 leading doctors, he obtained a comparable correlation, and he calculated that the odds against this being a matter of pure chance were of the order of 1 million to one.

Fortunately for us – though less happily for himself, for he subsequently became the

Above: traditionally Saturn, seen here in an illustration from the 15th-century codex *De sphaera*, exerts his influence over activities that require mature judgement. The French statistician Michel Gauquelin found the position of Saturn to be particularly significant in the horoscopes of scientists and doctors

Right: Karl Ernst Krafft, a Swiss astrologer, who moved to Germany in 1939 He correctly predicted that Hitler's life would be in danger between 7 and 10 November; in the event, Hitler made a narrow escape when a bomb exploded in a Munich beer cellar

target of much bitter criticism from the scientific establishment – Gauquelin decided to pursue this line of investigation further. From all over France he collected birth data for groups of eminent soldiers, politicians, writers, sportsmen and clerics. In every case, they showed a distinct correlation between the position of certain planets at birth with the subsequent career of the subject. Great soldiers, for instance, tended to have Mars or Jupiter just past the ascendant or the mid-heaven in their horoscopes. Gauquelin calculated that the probability that this was due to chance was as high as one in five million in certain groups.

Statistics and pulp romance

Even more remarkably, Gauquelin discovered that these significant results applied only to those who were truly successful. For instance, in a group of 1458 scientists who had never won a prize, made any important discovery or published more than run-of-the-mill research papers, there was no suggestion of significance in the position of Mars, Jupiter or Saturn at the time of birth.

Gauquelin's results provoked a great deal of interest in the French popular press, but for a long time the scientific community could not be persuaded to comment. At length Jean Porte, administrator of the Institute of Statistics, replied that the figures applied only to France: they revealed some kind of national characteristic that had nothing to do with astrology, and the same methods, applied to other countries, would produce quite different results. (Astrologers have pointed out the flaw in Porte's argument: if a different set of correlations for

Above: the French statistician Michel Gauquelin, who set out to disprove the standard beliefs of astrology. His research led him to a number of unexpected discoveries

Right: graphs showing the positions of Mars and Saturn, combined as a single line, in the horoscopes of 3305 scientists and 2048 musicians and painters. The graph for scientists is well above average at rising and at mid-heaven, whereas the graph for musicians and painters is significantly below average in these positions

Left: graphs showing the positions of Mars and Jupiter in the horoscopes of 3142 military leaders. The circle represents the average distribution that would be expected in such a large sample, and the solid line indicates the number of people with either planet at a particular angle in their horoscope. Significantly high departures from the average can be seen for planetary positions just above the horizon and just past mid-heaven

another country were discovered, it would only strengthen their belief that *all* planetary positions are significant in the horoscope.)

A committee of Belgian scientists had been set up in 1953 expressly to study paranormal phenomena; a member of this committee, Marcel Boll, commented:

Your conclusions are nothing but pulp-romances, the worst sort of proof, and the issue is without hope; for if you undertook the same inquiry in Great Britain, Germany, the USA or Russia you would come out with nothing but national idiosyncracies.

Challenged, Gauquelin and his wife set out on long journeys through Germany, Italy, Holland and Belgium to collect data from registers of birth. The results obtained after submission of the data to statistical analysis were substantially the same, with some interesting sidelights. It was found, for example, that Mars appeared in the significant positions for Italian soldiers far more frequently than for their German colleagues. Gauquelin

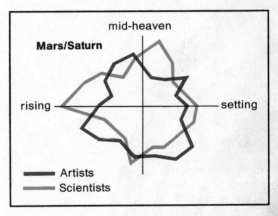

pointed out that one would expect Germans, *as a nation*, to be far more warlike than Italians; so that successful German soldiers were far less in need of a powerful Martian influence in their horoscopes, while the Italians would require (as it were) an overdose of militarism.

Science and the stars

Gauquelin and his wife collected birth data for more than 25,000 people. In the charts of 3305 scientists, Mars was found in one or other of the significant positions 666 times, where chance would have predicted 551 – the odds against this were computed at 500,000 to one. In the charts of 3142 military leaders, Mars was associated with the ascendant or the mid-heaven (with an additional small increase at the nadir, the point opposite the mid-heaven) in 634 cases, where chance indicated 524 – the odds being 1 million to one. In the same charts, Jupiter appeared significantly close to the two angles 644 times. And for 1485 athletes, Mars appeared at the significant angles 327 times, against a chance level of 248.

A number of control experiments were carried out to give a base with which to

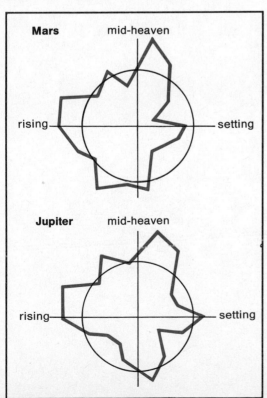

compare Gauquelin's findings. Groups of horoscopes selected at random gave the results expected according to chance; and further examination of the horoscopes of men in subordinate positions continued to reveal little divergence from the norm. It was only those who were successful in their professions who showed the significant planetary positions in their charts.

Analysing the survey results again,

Rising or setting	Significant high frequency	Average frequency	Significant low frequency
Mars	scientists doctors athletes executives	politicians actors journalists	writers painters musicians
Jupiter	team athletes soldiers politicians actors journalists playwrights	painters musicians writers	solo athletes scientists doctors
Saturn	scientists doctors	politicians soldiers	actors painters journalists writers
Moon	politicians writers	scientists doctors painters musicians journalists	athletes soldiers

Gauquelin spotted the occurrence of significantly low figures for planetary positions among certain specific groups. The table (above) summarises his analysis of his observations.

While he was pursuing these enquiries, Gauquelin was also looking out for any correlation with the position of the Sun – in other words, for some proof that the sign of the zodiac under which a person is born also affects their future development. He reported that he could find nothing of any statistical significance – but researchers in the USA and in Great Britain pursued this particular line of enquiry and obtained some interesting results. Because birth times are not generally recorded in these two countries, it was possible to work only with dates of birth, in which case the positions of the planets in the zodiac are known, but not their positions in relation to the ascendant or the mid-heaven.

Astrology and the professionals
In the USA, Edmund van Deusen processed 163,953 birth-dates for individuals born in the States and in Canada. In Great Britain, sociologist Joe Cooper, working with Dr Alan Smithers of the University of Bradford, studied some 35,000 birth-dates. Combining the results obtained by these researchers, we

get the following generalisations:

Soldiers: From 16,000 British army officers and 12,000 Americans, it was discovered that a significantly high proportion were born in late summer and early autumn, with peaks appearing in Leo and Scorpio.

Doctors: 6412 British and American doctors show above average figures for birth-dates in summer and autumn; and medical officers in the British army show a marked peaking in Scorpio.

Musicians: From 8932 British and American musicians and composers, an above average proportion were born in Sagittarius, Capricorn, Aquarius and Pisces.

Lawyers: 6677 American lawyers show a peak in Gemini.

Bankers: From 2696 bankers, a significant proportion have birth dates in Virgo.

Politicians: British politicians show a disproportionate tendency to be born in Aries.

Advertising executives and diplomats: The sample was from 7118 advertising agency men and 1834 diplomats. Both showed Gemini as the favoured sign of the zodiac.

Teachers: Van Deusen found that, of 5056 American school-teachers, a significant proportion were born in Leo or Virgo.

Librarians: 5111 American and Canadian librarians showed a marked trend toward Libra.

Authors: From a sample of 3927 British and American writers, a remarkably high proportion were born in Virgo.

Comedians: Cooper and Smithers found a marked tendency for comedians' birthdays to fall in Aquarius, Pisces, Aries, Taurus or Gemini.

It is important to remember that these statements represent statistical analysis of quite large samples. They are not to be explained away by the fact that the graph of births tends to show a peak in February and a trough in December; this kind of variation is allowed for in the calculations.

At about the same time that these findings were published, three British doctors made

Below: Dr Alan Smithers (left) and Joe Cooper studied data compiled from some 35,000 birth-dates, and obtained some remarkable findings

an analysis of some 28,000 cases of patients born between 1921 and 1955 who were admitted to psychiatric wards in 1970 and 1971. They found that 9 per cent more schizophrenics and 7 per cent more manic depressives had been born during the first three months of the year.

From this plethora of statistical information it begins to emerge that there may be more than a little truth in the suggestion advanced earlier, that a person's future development may (at the very least) be affected by the time of year in which he or she is born. Taken in conjunction with Gauquelin's work, it seems to lend strong support to the belief that the traditional tenets of astrology are founded in some kind of empirical data.

Emotional and neurotic

In 1977 a professional astrologer, Jeff Mayo, and one of Britain's most eminent psychologists, Professor Hans Eysenck, got together to investigate another of astrology's claims: that persons born in Cancer, Scorpio or Pisces tend to be unduly emotional and neurotic. Using a standard personality test that had been introduced by Eysenck in 1964, they found a definite correlation between the odd-numbered birth signs (Aries, Gemini, Leo, Libra, Sagittarius and Aquarius) and a tendency to extrovert behaviour; while the even-numbered signs (Taurus, Cancer, Virgo, Scorpio, Capricorn and Pisces) were associated with introversion. Furthermore, they showed that Cancer, Scorpio and Pisces – and, to Jeff Mayo's

Above: Professor Hans Eysenck, of the Institute of Psychiatry in the University of London, who has publicly declared his growing belief in astrology

considerable surprise, Aries – were statistically linked with emotional and neurotic personalities.

The most recent research seems to have gone even further toward popular beliefs about astrology than professional astrologers themselves would allow. It was pointed out in the first chapter in this series that astrologers did not accept the idea of 'compatibility' between those born in particular signs. But one of Eysenck's colleagues, Beverley Steffert, has been investigating the connection between Sun signs and happy marriages; and she believes that she has found that such marriages result when the couple involved were both born in either an even-numbered or an odd-numbered sign.

And there, for the moment, the case rests. Astrology is no longer merely a subject for popular columns in cheap newspapers, or for courses run by members of the mystic fringe for idle housewives. It is considered a suitable subject of study for medical men, statisticians and psychologists. Whether the movements of the planets provoke changes in the gravitational or magnetic fields of the solar system, or induce showers of cosmic radiation, and whether one or more of these influences has a profound (and predictable) effect upon the personality of those about to be born, only a great deal more research will reveal. But it seems true that we have underestimated the knowledge of the ancients: the magicians of Babylon knew rather more about the forces of destiny than we have, until now, given them credit for.

Astrological twins

When one looks at those who have achieved some degree of eminence in their professions, it is remarkable how many of them have related birth dates. Albert Einstein and Otto Hahn (below) were both born on 14 March 1879; operatic tenors Beniamino Gigli and Lauritz Melchior (far right) were both born on 20 March 1890. There are many

other examples; Hermann Göring and Alfred Rosenberg, two prominent members of the Nazi party, were born on the same day and died in the same prison on the same day. Even those whose birthdays fall on the same day, but are separated by a year or two, such as Vincent Price and Peter Cushing (centre) have remarkably similar careers.

Hitler and the holy lance

The holy lance, which pierced Christ's side at his crucifixion, became a talisman for the Teutonic warlords of Europe. In the 20th century it was plundered by Adolf Hitler, who knew its mystical significance all too well. FRANK SMYTH tells how the would-be conqueror of the world linked his destiny with the lance

IN THE STREETS OF VIENNA in 1913, a down-and-out former art student vainly tried to make a living by selling postcard-sized watercolours. Occasionally, driven off the streets by cold, he would wander through the corridors of the Hofburg Museum. Here he was particularly fascinated by a number of valuable pieces known as the Habsburg regalia. And among these the unprepossessing young vagrant, Adolf Hitler, paid special attention to the Holy Lance – reputed to be the spear that pierced Christ's side when he had given up the ghost on the cross.

The legend of the Holy Lance takes its origin from John 19:33–37:

But when they came to Jesus, and saw that he was dead already, they brake not his legs: But one of the soldiers with a spear pierced his side, and forthwith came there out blood and water. And he that saw it bare record, and his record is true: and he knoweth that he saith true, that ye might believe. For these things were done that the scripture should be fulfilled, A bone of him shall not be broken. And again another scripture saith, They shall look on him whom they pierced.

The verse following this tells how Joseph of Arimathaea gained permission to take the body of Jesus and, helped by Nicodemus, laid it in a tomb on the night of Good Friday.

Other oral and written traditions, beginning with the earliest Christians and continuing to the Middle Ages, depict the rich Jewish philanthropist as obsessed with the artefacts associated with the dead Christ. He is said to have preserved the cross itself, the nails, the crown of thorns, and the shroud from which Christ rose on the third day. Through clues left by Joseph, Helena, mother of the first Christian emperor, Constantine, was able to rediscover these relics.

But even before Christ's death, according to the same traditions, Joseph had begun collecting: after the last supper he took charge of the cup in which Jesus had consecrated the bread and wine. After the resurrection, Joseph kept this cup alongside the spear of John's Gospel: the Holy Grail and the Holy Lance.

Joseph's subsequent travels with the Grail

Far left: the blade of the Habsburg spear, reputed to be the lance that pierced Christ's side while he was on the cross. Because it was a holy relic, the iron blade has been extensively repaired with gold and silver during its long history. It is now bound together with wire and an inscribed 'sleeve'

Left: a Roman soldier confirms that Christ is dead by plunging a spear into him, in a painting by Rubens. According to tradition, it was revealed to the soldier at this moment that Christ was truly the Son of God, and the spear acquired enduring magical potency

Right: just one face in the crowds of Germans who exulted at the outbreak of the First World War: Adolf Hitler, poverty-stricken and obscure, but dreaming already of leading the Nordic 'master race' to supremacy

Below: by selling watercolours like this, Hitler scratched a living in Vienna in 1913

and the Lance are the subject of folk tales and legends in almost every country in Europe. In Britain he is said to have hidden the Grail at Glastonbury. Afterwards he thrust his staff into the ground, where it sprouted to become the still-surviving Glastonbury Thorn, which blooms only at Christmas.

Romantic writers, beginning with the French poet Chrétien de Troyes in about 1180, bound up the fate of the Holy Grail and the Holy Lance with the adventures of King Arthur and the Knights of the Round Table, notably with Lancelot, Gawain and Perceval.

Alongside these stories – themselves based on Celtic tradition and scraps of historical fact – there ran a thin thread of evidence that the Lance, at least, had survived the centuries, passed down sometimes through good hands, sometimes through unworthy ones. With its ownership came power, to be used for great good or for terrible evil.

At least four 'Holy Lances' existed in Europe during the early part of the present century. Perhaps the best-known was in the keeping of the Vatican, although the Roman Catholic Church seems to have regarded it as no more than a curio. Certainly no preternatural powers were claimed for it by the papal authorities.

A second lance was kept in Paris, where it had been taken by St Louis in the 13th century, after his return from the crusades in Palestine.

Another lance, preserved in Cracow, Poland, was merely a copy of the Habsburg lance. The latter probably had the best pedigree of them all. It had been discovered at Antioch in 1098, during the first crusade, but mystery – and possibly imagination – obscured the manner of its finding. Crusaders had mounted a successful siege of the city and had taken control, when a more heavily armed band of Saracens rode up and turned the tables, shutting up the crusaders within the walls in their turn. After three weeks water and food were running low and surrender seemed the only course. Then a

priest claimed to have had a miraculous vision of the Holy Lance, buried in the church of St Peter. When excavations at the spot revealed the iron spearhead, the crusaders were filled with a new zeal and rode out to rout their attackers.

Germanic tradition, somewhat at odds with these dates, claimed the Habsburg lance had in fact been carried as a talisman in the ninth century by Charlemagne through 47 victorious campaigns. It had also endowed him with clairvoyant powers. Only when he accidentally dropped it did Charlemagne die.

The lance later passed into the possession of Heinrich the Fowler, who founded the royal house of the Saxons and drove the Poles eastwards – a foreshadowing, Hitler may have thought in later years, of his own destiny. After passing through the hands of five Saxon monarchs, it fell into the possession of the succeeding Hohenstauffens of Swabia. One of the most outstanding of this line was Frederick Barbarossa, born in 1123. Before his death 67 years later Barbarossa had conquered Italy and driven the Pope himself into exile; again, Hitler may well have admired the brutal harshness coupled with charismatic personality that drove Barbarossa to success. Like Charlemagne, however, Barbarossa made the mistake of dropping the lance as he waded a stream in Sicily. He died within minutes of this event.

The fascination of the spear

This was the legend of the weapon now among the Habsburg regalia, which so fascinated the young Hitler. He spent his first visit to the lance studying its every detail. It was just over a foot (30 centimetres) long, tapering to a slender, leaf-shaped point, and at some time the blade had been grooved to admit a nail – allegedly one of those used in the crucifixion. This had been bound into place with gold wire. The spear had been broken, and the two halves were joined by a sheath of silver, while two gold crosses had been inlaid into the base, near the haft.

The evidence of Hitler's personal fascination with the Habsburg lance rests on the testimony of Dr Walter Johannes Stein, a mathematician, economist and occultist who claimed to have met the future Führer just before the First World War. Stein, a native of Vienna, was born in 1891, the son of a rich barrister. He was to be a polymath and an intellectual adventurer until his death in 1957. He took a first degree in science and a doctorate in psychophysical research at the University of Vienna. He became expert in archaeology, early Byzantine art and medieval history; in the First World War, as an officer in the Austrian Army, he was decorated for gallantry.

In 1928 he published an eccentric pamphlet, *World history in the light of the Holy Grail*, which was circulated in Germany, Holland and Britain. Just five years after that Reichsführer Heinrich Himmler ordered that he be pressed into service with the Nazi 'Occult Bureau', but Stein escaped to Britain.

The Second World War found him in the guise of British intelligence agent. After helping to obtain the plans for 'Operation Sealion' – Hitler's projected invasion of Britain – he acted as adviser to Winston Churchill on the German leader's occult involvements.

Stein never published his own memoirs, but before his death he befriended an ex-Sandhurst commando officer, then a journalist, Trevor Ravenscroft. Using Stein's notes and conversations, Ravenscroft published a book, *Spear of destiny*, in 1972, which first brought Hitler's fascination with the Habsburg spear to public attention.

What hold could the Holy Lance, a Christian symbol, have on the violently anti-Christian ex-Roman Catholic Adolf Hitler? Already he was given to violent anti-Semitic rantings, and already he was a devout student of Friedrich Nietzsche's *Anti-Christ*, with its condemnation of Christianity as 'the ultimate Jewish consequence'.

Part of the answer lay in a medieval occult tradition regarding the history of the Holy Lance. As the Gospel of John describes, the Roman soldier who pierced Christ had unwittingly fulfilled the Old Testament prophecies (that Christ's bones would not be broken). Had he not done as he did, the destiny of mankind would have been different. According to both Matthew and Mark the true nature of Christ was revealed to the soldier, said to be named Gaius Cassius Longinus, at that moment: 'And

Above: Charlemagne, King of the Franks, became Holy Roman Emperor in AD 800. One of the legends that have grown up around him says that he owed his success in war to the Holy Lance

Below: the triumphal entry of Hitler into Vienna in March 1938. One of the Führer's first acts was to order the removal to Germany of the Habsburg treasure, which included the Holy Lance

when the centurion, which stood over against him, saw that he so cried out, and gave up the ghost, he said, Truly this man was the Son of God.' (Mark 15:39.)

To the mind of the occultist, an instrument used for such momentous purpose would itself become the focus of magical power. And as Richard Cavendish succinctly puts it, speaking of the Grail and the Lance in his book *King Arthur and the Grail*:

A thing is not sacred because it is good. It is sacred because it contains mysterious and awesome power. It is as potent for good or evil as a huge charge of electricity. If it is tampered with, however compelling and understandable the motive, the consequences may be catastrophic for entirely innocent people.

According to Stein, Hitler was fully aware of this concept as early as 1912: indeed it was through Hitler's obsession with the legend of the lance and its power as a 'magic wand' that the two men met. In the summer of 1912 Dr Stein purchased an edition of *Parsival*, a Grail romance by the 13th-century German poet Wolfram von Eschenbach, from an occult bookseller in Vienna. It was full of scribbled marginal commentaries displaying a combination of occult learning and pathological racism. On the flyleaf its previous owner had signed his name: Adolf Hitler. Through the bookseller Stein traced Hitler and spent many hours with him, appalled but fascinated. Although it was to be years before the poverty-stricken postcard painter took his first steps on the road to power, there was already an evil charisma about the man. Through all the tortuous windings of his discourse one obsession stood out clearly: he had a mystic destiny to fulfil and, according to Stein, the lance held the key.

Hitler described to Stein how the spear had acquired a special significance for him:

> I slowly became aware of a mighty presence around it, the same awesome presence which I had experienced inwardly on those rare occasions in my life when I had sensed that a great destiny awaited me... a window in the future was opened up to me through which I saw in a single flash of illumination a future event by which I knew beyond contradiction that the blood in my veins would one day become the vessel of the Folk-Spirit of my people.

Hitler never revealed the nature of his 'vision'; but Stein believed that he had seen himself a quarter of a century later, in the Heldenplatz outside the Hofburg Museum, addressing Austrian Nazis and ordinary, bewildered Viennese. There, on 14 March 1938, the German Führer was to announce his annexation of Austria into the German Reich – and to give the order to carry the Habsburg regalia off to Nuremberg, spiritual home of the Nazi movement.

A curious priority

Taking possession of the treasure was a curious priority in view of the fact that Hitler despised the house of Habsburg as traitors to the Germanic race. Nevertheless on 13 October the spear and the other items of the regalia were loaded onto an armoured train with an ss guard and taken across the German border. They were lodged in the hall of St Catherine's Church, where Hitler proposed to set up a Nazi war museum. Stein believed that when Hitler had the lance in his possession, his latent ambitions for world conquest began to grow and flourish.

If Hitler's knowledge of the Habsburg spear's history was as extensive as Stein claimed, he must have been aware of the legends concerning the fate of Charlemagne, Barbarossa and others who had wielded it as a weapon, only to perish when it fell from their grasp. The legend seemed to be confirmed by a chilling coincidence that marked the end of his connection with the Lance.

After heavy Allied bombing in October 1944, during which Nuremberg suffered extensive damage, Hitler ordered the spear, along with the rest of the Habsburg regalia, to be buried in a specially constructed vault.

Left: the closing scene of *Parsifal*, Wagner's last opera. Hitler was fascinated by the legend on which the opera is based. Here the enchantress Kundry, redeemed from a life of evil, dies as Parsifal takes the Holy Grail from its shrine. He holds the Holy Lance, which, having been used to work evil by the black magician Klingsor, is an instrument of blessing in the hands of the virtuous Parsifal

Below: the Luitpold Arena in Nuremberg, scene of the Nazis' most spectacular pre-war rallies, saw an informal 'march past' by victorious US soldiers in April 1945 (inset). In the ruins of the shattered city the Holy Lance, with other war booty, was found in a bombproof vault

Six months later the American Seventh Army had surrounded the ancient city, which was defended by 22,000 ss troops, 100 Panzers and 22 regiments of artillery. For four days the veteran American Thunderbird Division battered at this formidable defence until, on 20 April 1945 – Hitler's 56th birthday – the victorious Stars and Stripes was hoisted over the rubble.

During the next few days, while American troops rounded up Nazi survivors and began the long process of interrogating them, Company c of the us Army's Third Military Government Regiment, under their commander Lieutenant William Horn, were detailed to search for the Habsburg treasure. By chance a shell had made their task easier by blowing away brickwork and revealing the entrance to the vault. After some difficulty with the vault's steel doors, Lieutenant Horn entered the underground chamber and peered through the dusty gloom. There, lying on a bed of faded red velvet, was the fabled spear of Longinus. Lieutenant Horn reached out and took possession of the spear on behalf of the United States government. It was the afternoon of 30 April 1945. That much is recorded history.

And however sceptical may be the critics – about Walter Stein, the occult in general and the Holy Lance legends in particular – it is also historical fact that a few hundred miles away in a bunker in Berlin, Adolf Hitler chose that evening on which to take a pistol and shoot himself.

Legions of hell

The Nazi Party's rise to power has been attributed to occult practice. And Adolf Hitler himself was undoubtedly fascinated by the 'black arts'. This chapter explains how and why this bizarre association developed

IN THE LATE SUMMER of 1940, as the battle of Britain was drawing to its close, Toby O'Brien, then press secretary to Winston Churchill, had an inspiration. He was sitting in his bath one morning when the words of a coarse comic song began to form 'unbidden' in his mind. He repeated his composition over lunch later that day to a group of high-ranking British officers in Whitehall. They were convulsed with mirth. Some of them wrote it down, while others memorised it. Within weeks it had filtered through the ranks and was on the lips of squadron leaders and squaddies, admirals and artificers. Sung to the tune of 'Colonel Bogey' it went:

> Hitler, he only had one ball;
> Göring had two but very small.
> Himmler was very similar,
> But poor old Goebbels
> Had no balls at all.

Toby O'Brien certainly did not believe his composition was accurate: precious little was known about the sexual endowments or habits of the Führer. But when Russian military surgeons examined Hitler's charred remains in the Berlin bunker in May 1945, they discovered that Hitler was indeed mon-orchid: he possessed but one testicle. It was a bizarre and extreme coincidence.

But Hitler's defect may have had a profound significance for the development of his occult ideas. According to Dr Walter Stein,

The swastika became the official insignia of the Nazi Party (below: banners at a rally at Nuremberg in 1933) in the 1920s. Sitting on a white disc with a red background, it was a striking symbol, which to Adolf Hitler (right) represented all the ideals of the nationalist movement. Many have seen Hitler's decision to reverse the symbol – to use a 'left-handed' swastika rather than the traditional 'right-handed' one – as an indication of his sinister leanings. And, once a symbol of good fortune, the swastika is now seen as the embodiment of evil itself

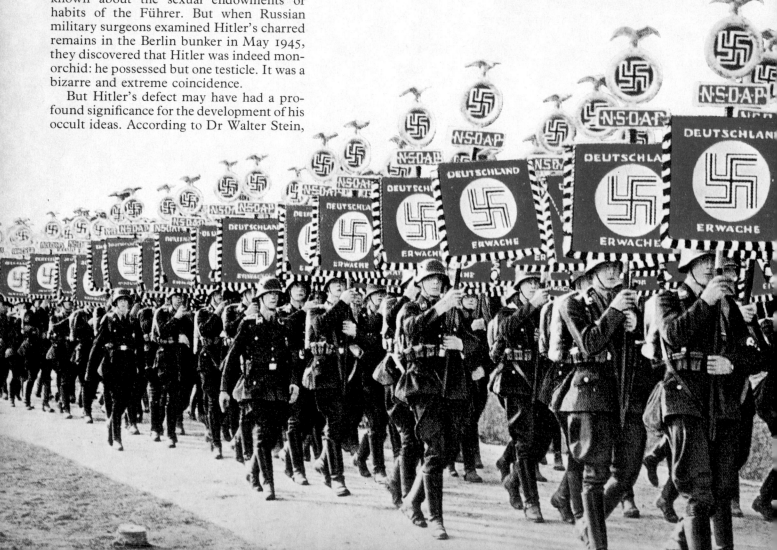

whose observations on his personal conversations with Hitler in Vienna formed the basis of Trevor Ravenscroft's *The spear of destiny*, Hitler had, as early as 1912, formed a passion for the music of Richard Wagner – particularly for *Parsifal*, which praised Teutonic knighthood and exalted the Aryan race. Soon Hitler discovered Wagner's source: the medieval poetry of Wolfram von Eschenbach. In fact it was through buying a copy of Eschenbach's *Parsival* that had once belonged to Hitler that Dr Stein met him. Dr Stein was impressed by the meticulousness of the marginal notes, though simultaneously appalled by the pathological race hatred that they showed. Among them appeared numerous references to the character Klingsor, whom Hitler apparently identified with the notorious ninth-century tyrant Landulph II of Capua.

Landulph's avaricious grasping for power had led him to study the black arts, and it was for these practices that he was excommunicated in AD 875. But one other fact must have given Hitler a sense of identity with the ninth-century 'Führer'. Landulph seems to have been either partly or totally castrated: Eschenbach described him as 'the man who was smooth between the legs'.

We know that Hitler was easily influenced as a youth, avidly soaking up the ideas of

Below: Toby O'Brien who, in 1940, penned an unwittingly accurate lampoon against Adolf Hitler

Long before Guido von List (below) adopted the swastika as the emblem of his neo-pagan movement in Germany in the late 19th century, the 'crooked cross' was a widespread symbol of good luck, of life and of energy. The swastikas on this figure (right), on the handle of a bucket found in the 9th-century ship-burial at Oseberg, Norway, represent the hammers of Thor, god of thunder and of war. Those on the plinth of this statue of Kali (above right), the hideous aspect of the Hindu Goddess, signify a life-giving regenerating force

those – Wagner and Nietzsche, for instance – who impressed him. Landulph's power mania and his unfortunate anatomical similarity to himself must have struck the young Adolf, and there is reason to suspect that Landulph's black magic did so too. Another source gives us a very clear indication that Hitler was impressed by magical symbolism from the beginning of his political career.

Throughout the latter half of the 19th century, German pseudo-intellectual circles had been obsessed with a movement compounded of pagan ritual and notions of Nordic purity invented by a man named Guido von List. Born in 1848, the son of a

rich trader in leather goods and top boots – pointers, perhaps, to things to come – von List had renounced his Catholicism when he was 14 with a solemn oath that he would one day build a temple to Woden (also called Odin), war god of Scandinavian mythology.

By the 1870s von List had a sizeable group of followers, dedicated to observing 'pagan' feasts at the solstices and equinoxes. In 1875 they attracted attention to themselves by worshipping the Sun as Baldur, the Nordic god, slain in battle, who rose from the dead. The rite was held on a hilltop near Vienna, and concluded with von List burying eight wine bottles carefully laid out in the shape of a swastika.

The swastika had been a widespread symbol of good fortune from earliest times and among all nations; it had been found on Chinese, Mongolian and American Indian artefacts, was used by the ancient Greeks as a pottery decoration, and by medieval architects as a border design for stained glass windows. Its name in Middle English, *fylfot*, is said to mean 'fill foot', since it was a device used for 'filling the foot' of windows. 'Swastika' stems from the Sanskrit *Su asti*, which means, literally translated, 'Good, he is.' In fact the swastika, with its arms 'trailing' as if the whole pattern were spinning clockwise, symbolised the Sun, the powers of light.

In the 1920s, when the National Socialist movement was in its infancy, Hitler asked for designs to be submitted for an easily recognisable symbol, akin to the hammer and sickle of the Russian communists. Friedrich

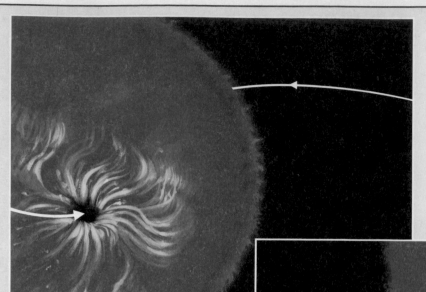

a moon with the Earth, some 13,000 years ago, he claimed, caused the disappearance of Atlantis – the continent that, the Nazis believed, was the original home of the Aryan race.

Himmler was particularly impressed with Hörbiger's theories, and a treatise on the cosmic ice theory was published as one of a series of handbooks for the SA (the paramilitary wing of the Nazi Party). And Hitler himself declared that he would build an observatory in his home town of Linz, dedicated to the three great cosmologists: Copernicus, Kepler – and Hanns Hörbiger.

A world of ice

How did the cosmological theories of a blacksmith-turned-engineer become a mainstay of the Nazi world view?

The man in question was one Hanns Hörbiger (far right), who believed that, among the 'cosmic building stuff' that makes up the Universe, there exists water in its 'cosmic form' – ice. This ice forms itself into large blocks that orbit young stars. Ignoring Kepler's laws of motion, which state that orbiting bodies travel in ellipses, Hörbiger argued that these blocks of ice follow a spiral path, so that they eventually collide with the star (above), causing an enormous explosion. The star ejects a molten mass of rotating matter (above right), which forms a new solar system (right).

Hörbiger's belief that planets follow a spiral path led him to suggest that there were originally four moons orbiting the Earth, of which our present Moon is the only remaining one. The last collision of

Krohn, a Sternberg dentist who was also an occultist, suggested a swastika on a white disc with a red background – red for blood and the social ideal, white for nationalism and purity of race, and the swastika for 'the struggle for victory of Aryan man'.

Hitler was delighted but for one detail – the traditional 'right-handed' swastika was to be reversed to form what the writer Francis King terms 'an evocation of evil, spiritual devolution and black magic'.

Dr Krohn fully realised Hitler's intention in changing the ancient sign, for he was a member of the *Germanenorden* – German Order – which, with the Thule Society, had taken over where von List's rather amateurish organisation had left off in the years

before the First World War. Both societies – which eventually became almost interchangeable in ideas and even membership – were originally composed of the German officer class and professions, who were convinced of a massive international Jewish conspiracy backed up by occult practices. To counter this they established their own Nordic occult-based freemasonry, complete with elaborate rituals and robes, Viking helmets and swords. More importantly, the Thule Society – which took its name from the fabled land of Ultima Thule, a sort of paradise on Earth – began to recruit new members from the lower classes and disseminated anti-Semitic material in its various newspapers, one of which, the

Völkischer Beobachter, eventually became the official journal of the Nazi Party.

There is no doubt that Hitler, both in his down-and-out days in Vienna and later, as leader of the rising Nazi Party in the 1920s and 1930s, was constantly fascinated by 'fringe' occult theories. One of these was the lunatic 'World Ice Theory', a complicated set of ideas propagated by an Austrian engineer named Hanns Hörbiger (1860–1931). He claimed that the planets had been created by the collision of stars such as the Sun with huge chunks of ice. Hörbiger claimed that his system enabled him to forecast the weather accurately. Some occult writers, notably Pauwels and Bergier in their *Dawn of magic*, have suggested that Hörbiger's forecasts influenced Hitler's disastrous Russian campaign.

Latterly, Hitler became obsessed with map dowsing – swinging a pendulum over a map to find hidden objects. The topic was brought to the attention of Hitler's aides by an architect named Ludwig Straniak, yet another amateur occultist. Straniak demonstrated to German naval officers his apparent ability to pinpoint the whereabouts of their ships at sea, simply by dangling a pendulum over an admiralty chart. They were particularly impressed when he located the pocket battleship *Prinz Eugen*, at that time on a secret mission.

The 'black magicians'

Hitler's involvement with astrology, and prediction in general, has been much debated. It has even been claimed that he had powers of precognition, which allowed him to foresee the lack of opposition to his invasions of Austria and Czechoslovakia. But Hitler's real talent was as a masterly judge of the European political mood – and even this intuition deserted him when he decided to invade Poland in 1939.

Josef Goebbels, propaganda minister, used astrology cleverly but cynically – quoting Nostradamus, for instance, in support of Nazi domination. Hitler and, in particular, ss chief Himmler took astrology seriously.

In view of this varied preoccupation with the occult, many have suggested that, among high-ranking Nazis, Hitler and Himmler at least were in a real sense 'black magicians'. However, one great question confronts those who claim this. Why, when the Nazis rose to power, were occult writings and practices so rigorously stamped upon – for so they were?

In 1934 the first move was made when the Berlin police issued a ban on all forms of fortune-telling, from fairground palmists to society astrologers. That the orders came from central headquarters is certain, for the police officers who carried out the orders were extremely confused as to the intention behind them. They both impounded 'innocent' books and let go books of magic spells and similar works.

Next came a general suppression of all

Top: the German pocket battleship *Prinz Eugen*, which occultist Ludwig Straniak located simply by swinging a pendulum over a map. After hearing of Straniak's impressive demonstrations, Hitler himself became interested in – then obsessed with – map dowsing

Above: Josef Goebbels, Hitler's minister for propaganda and enlightenment. Although no believer in the occult, he recognised Hitler's fascination for the subject and skilfully used it as a psychological weapon to further the Nazi cause among the German people

occult groups, even – to the chagrin and surprise of members – the German Order and the Thule Society. Both these contained many Nazis, of course, but even for these there was no exemption. For instance, Jörg Lanz von Liebenfels, whose writings inspired much of the German racial mystique, and who boasted that by introducing Hitler to occult groups he had been his 'guru', was told that he must not publish occult works in future.

With the sole exceptions of 'inner party members', such as certain of Himmler's personal ss aides, occultists of all shades had been done away with or driven underground in German-occupied countries by 1940.

The answer to the enigma has been pointed out by such writers as Francis King and J. H. Brennan. They argue that in regimes that in some ways are analogous with Hitler's – Mao's China, for instance, and Stalin's Russia – there was no such systematic weeding out of occultists. True, Stalin pounced on freemasons, cabalists, and the like, but only because they were 'secret societies' *per se*, not because of their 'magical' activities. In China, even after the Cultural Revolution, seers and astrologers were frowned upon as superstitious, but nothing desperate was done against them. They were more mocked at than persecuted. Authoritarian regimes do not seem to fear magical practices as such.

But Nazi Germany had to trample down 'freelance' occultists, because it was in effect trampling down its own rivals – in much the same way that Trotskyites suffered under Stalin.

There was only one occult movement permissible under the Third Reich, and it was hidden deep in its coils. It was led by the supreme magus, Adolf Hitler, and his acolyte, Heinrich Himmler: both of them powerful black magicians.

Was Hitler a black magician?

Adolf Hitler had an extraordinary ability to influence others. But was his charisma due to sheer strength of personality, to hypnotic skills – or to diabolical magic? Could he literally bewitch people?

THE GOAL OF EVERY MAGICIAN is power over natural forces. He aims to seize the infinite forces of the cosmos and wield them like a sword in his own service. A magician who seeks this power for his own ends, without the wish to serve any higher good, is a 'black' magician. According to most magical schools of thought he pays a high price in the end for his pride. Often he becomes possessed by the spirits he calls upon and is destroyed by them. In the view of several occultists, Adolf Hitler was a powerful black magician.

According to one of Hitler's few friends from his early years in Linz, his personal power had developed by the time he was 15 years old, and very startling it was. On one occasion:

Adolf Hitler stood in front of me and gripped my hands and held them tight. . . . The words did not come smoothly from his mouth as they usually did, but rather erupted, hoarse and raucous. . . . It was as if another being

Below: Karl Dönitz, commander of the U-boat fleet, met Hitler as infrequently as possible, because he felt the Führer's 'powers of suggestion' impaired his judgement

spoke out of his body and moved him as much as it moved me. It was not at all a case of a speaker carried away by his own words. On the contrary; I rather felt as though he himself listened with astonishment and emotion to what burst forth from him with elemental force. . . .

The writer of this excerpt was August Kubizek. He was describing a midnight walk in 1904 with the 15-year-old Hitler following a performance of Wagner's opera *Rienzi*, which tells the story of the meteoric rise and fall of a Roman tribune. Hitler's inspired speech concerned the future of Germany and 'a mandate which, one day, he would receive from the people to lead them from servitude. . . .'

According to Kubizek, Hitler spent a great deal of time studying oriental mysticism, astrology, hypnotism, Germanic mythology and other aspects of occultism. By 1909 he had made contact with Dr Jörg Lanz von Liebenfels, a former Cistercian monk who, two years previously, had opened a temple of the 'Order of New Templars' at the tumbledown Werfenstein Castle on the banks of the Danube.

Von Liebenfels had assumed his

aristocratic-sounding name: he was born plain Adolf Lanz and came of solid bourgeois stock. His following was small but wealthy. A disciple of Guido von List (see page 58), he flew a swastika flag from his battlements, performed ritual magic and ran a magazine entitled *Ostara*, a propaganda journal of occultism and race mysticism, to which the young Hitler became an avid subscriber. In 1932 Von Liebenfels wrote to a colleague:

Hitler is one of our pupils . . . you will one day experience that he, and through him we, will one day be victorious and develop a movement that will make the world tremble.

The Italian dictator Benito Mussolini visited Hitler in Germany in 1943, mentally exhausted and deeply depressed. Yet Hitler's influence and the force of his personality were so strong that, according to Josef Goebbels, after only four days in his company Mussolini underwent a complete transformation

I purposely went very seldom to his headquarters, for I had the feeling that I would best preserve my power of initiative and also because, after several days at headquarters, I always had the feeling that I had to disengage myself from his powers of suggestion. . . . I was doubtless more fortunate than his staff, who were constantly exposed to his power and personality.

In his diary for 7 April 1943 Josef Goebbels recorded a remarkable instance of Hitler's use of the force of his personality. The Italian dictator Mussolini had visited Germany in a state of deep depression and mental exhaustion:

By putting every ounce of nervous energy into the effort he [Hitler] succeeded in pushing Mussolini back onto the rails. In those four days the Duce underwent a complete change. When he got out of the train on his arrival the Führer thought he looked like a broken old man. When he left again he was in high fettle, ready for anything.

In March 1936 Hitler made a statement that precisely summed up the impressions of those who knew him best: 'I am going the way Providence dictates,' he said, 'with the assurance of a sleepwalker.' It was as if something else – not his own mind and soul – was in charge of his every action.

This ruling spirit, if such it was, was not always kind to its host. Hitler's frantic,

One of this ex-monk's pronouncements was that human breeding farms should be set up 'in order to eradicate Slavic and Alpine elements from Germanic heredity', prefiguring Himmler's idea of an SS stud farm by over 20 years.

By the onset of the First World War, Hitler seems to have developed an unshakable conviction of his own high destiny: as a messenger at the front he took enormous risks as if he knew that fate would not allow him to die just yet. By the time the war ended he had developed that curious, impersonal power over those around him that was to stand him in such good stead until late in his career.

Again and again the idea that Hitler was 'possessed' was echoed in the writings of those who knew him. His uncanny hold over individuals was a bugbear to those in the highest echelons of the state. Once, for example, Dr Hjalmar Schacht, Hitler's financial wizard, asked Hermann Göring to speak to Hitler about a minor point of economic policy. But in Hitler's presence Göring found himself unable to raise the matter. He told Schacht: 'I often make up my mind to say something to him, but when I meet him face to face my heart sinks. . . .'

Grand Admiral Karl Dönitz was so conscious of the Führer's influence that he avoided his company so as to leave his own judgement unimpaired:

Above: children born in the Steinhöring *Lebensborn*, one of many SS breeding farms set up by Heinrich Himmler to ensure the production of a Nordic 'super race'

Left: Hitler's ability to mesmerise individuals and groups, as at this informal gathering of his followers in Munich in the mid 1930s, led many to believe that he had supernatural powers

screaming rages, when he would literally froth at the mouth and fall to the floor, are well-documented. Even more frightening is the account given by his confidant Hermann Rauschning in his book *Hitler speaks*:

He wakes up in the night, screaming and in convulsions. He calls for help, and appears to be half paralysed. He is seized with panic that makes him tremble until the bed shakes. He utters confused and unintelligible sounds, gasping as if on the point of suffocation. . . .

Hitler was not certain at all times of his

Deputy Reichsführer of the SS – the *Schutzstaffel*, or protective force, a body of about 300 men dedicated to bodyguard duties.

But by 1933 Himmler had built up the SS to such a strength that he was confident enough to purge it – retaining only men of the finest 'Germanic' physical characteristics and insisting that its officers should be able to show a non-Jewish ancestry going back to 1750. After a lengthy quasi-mystical novitiate, recruits were given a ceremonial dagger and permission to wear the full black uniform of the SS, complete with silver death's head. Thereafter they were obliged to attend what Francis King, author of *Satan and the swastika*, describes as 'neo-pagan ceremonies of a specifically SS religion devised by Himmler and clearly derived from his interest in occultism and the worship of Woden.'

Himmler had abandoned his Catholic faith for spiritualism, astrology and mesmerism in his late teens. He was convinced that he was the reincarnation of Heinrich the Fowler, founder of the Saxon royal house, who died in 936. All these elements were incorporated into his SS 'religion'.

Himmler devised new festivals to take the place of such Christian events as Christmas and Easter, he wrote out baptism and marriage ceremonies – though he believed polygamy would best serve the interests of the SS élite – and he even issued instructions on the correct manner of committing suicide.

The centre of the SS 'cult' became the castle of Wewelsburg in Westphalia, which Himmler bought as a ruin in 1934 and rebuilt over the next 11 years at a cost of 13 million

'guiding spirit's' intentions. He suffered from a horror of ill omens. Albert Speer, who became Hitler's personal architect and finally Germany's minister of war production, recounted an incident in October 1933 that shook Hitler's confidence more than anything up to that point had been able to do. He was laying the foundation stone of the House of German Art in Munich, which had been designed by his friend Paul Ludwig Troost and which Hitler felt embodied the highest ideals of Teutonic architecture. As he tapped the stone with a silver hammer, the instrument shattered to fragments in his hand. For almost three months Hitler was wrapped in morbid gloom; then on 21 January 1934 Troost died. Hitler's relief was immediate. He told Speer: 'When that hammer shattered I knew at once it was an evil omen. Something is going to happen, I thought. Now we know why the hammer broke. The architect was destined to die.'

Sorcerer's apprentice

Josef Goebbels pretended to an interest in the occult and in astrology in order to please the Führer – even going so far as to gain proficiency in drawing up a horoscope. Rudolf Hess may have dabbled in occult matters. But there was only one true 'sorcerer's apprentice' in Hitler's inner circle.

Heinrich Himmler was born of middle-class parents in Munich in 1900. A weak, pale and characterless youth, whose defective eyesight compelled him to wear thick-lensed spectacles, Himmler became a fervent Nazi in the early 1920s and was appointed secretary to the Nazi Party propaganda office in Lower Bavaria. There in his little office he sat and talked to a portrait of Hitler on the wall, long before he met the man himself. Although he had indubitable organising ability, Himmler's appearance made him something of a laughing stock, and it was almost jocularly that Hitler appointed him

marks. The central banqueting hall contained a vast round table with 13 throne-like seats to accommodate Himmler and 12 of his closest 'apostles' – making, as some occult writers have pointed out, a coven of 13. Beneath this hall was a 'Hall of the Dead', where plinths stood around a stone table. As each member of the inner circle of the SS died, his coat of arms would be burned and, together with his ashes, placed in an urn on one of these plinths for veneration.

In this slightly ludicrous atmosphere of theatricality, Himmler instigated the systematic genocide carried out by the Third Reich in its last years. Millions of Jews, gypsies, homosexuals and others who did not

conform to the ideas of the Führer and of himself were slaughtered. Many of the atrocities were prompted by Himmler's bizarre theories. For example, his belief in the power of 'animal heat' led to experiments in which victims were exposed in freezing cold water and then revived – if they were fortunate – by being placed between the naked bodies of prostitutes. On another occasion, he decided that statistics should be collected of the measurements of Jewish skulls; but only the skulls of the newly dead would be suitable, so hundreds of people were decapitated.

Less horrific but equally insane were SS researches into the Rosicrucian movement, the symbolism of the suppression of the Irish harp in Ulster, the occult significance of Gothic towers and the Eton top hat, and the magical power of the bells of Oxford, which, Himmler decided, had put a charm on the Luftwaffe, preventing it inflicting serious damage on the city.

The occult writer J. H. Brennan has gone so far as to suggest that Himmler was a 'nonperson', a zombie without mind or soul of its own, drawing power from Hitler like a psychic leech. Francis King has pointed out that the huge Nuremberg rallies, presided

Above: the castle of Wewelsburg in north-west Germany was bought by Heinrich Himmler (top) in 1934 and became the temple of his SS cult. The presence of the gypsy caravan so close to the Nazi shrine would not be tolerated for long, for gypsies were among the millions of non-Aryans exterminated by Himmler in his attempt to 'purify' the Germanic race

over by Hitler at his most 'possessed', fulfil the conditions necessary for what some witch cults describe as a 'cone of power': searchlights pierced the night sky in a conical pattern above vast crowds, which generated a giant surge of emotion centred on the strutting figure of Hitler.

But if Himmler could be magically influenced for evil he could also be influenced for good in the same way. The unlikely instrument of this good was a plump blond masseur and occultist named Felix Kersten. He had been trained in osteopathy and allied skills by a mysterious Chinese doctor named Ko. Dr Ko was also an occultist and mystic, who apparently developed latent psychic powers in Kersten. Success and fame came to Kersten, and he was ordered to attend Himmler, who suffered from chronic stomach cramps, in 1938. Thereafter the SS chief was almost totally dependent on Kersten, who was able on a number of occasions to save hundreds of Jewish lives by his hold on Himmler's mind. A postwar investigating commission concluded that Kersten's service to mankind and to the cause of peace was 'so outstanding that no comparable precedent could be found for it in history.'

Awesome power

By what appears to have been sheer force of will, for instance, Kersten persuaded Himmler on more than one occasion to defer the extermination of concentration camp prisoners. Kersten would 'worry away like a terrier' until Himmler dropped the whole business. The masseur also managed, with at least partial success, to influence Himmler through deliberate misinterpretation of horoscopes – in which Himmler believed more fervently, perhaps, than Hitler himself.

From the middle of 1942 Kersten was busy sowing in Himmler's mind the notion that he should try to make a separate peace with the Western Allies; though he drew the Reichsführer to the brink on several occasions, he was unable to counteract the awesome power wielded by Hitler himself.

As Francis King has pointed out, Hitler's policies as Germany approached its collapse tallied exactly with what could be expected of a black magician's pact with evil powers. The essence of such a pact lies in sacrifice: an orgy of blood and destruction.

'Losses,' Hitler told Field Marshal Walther von Reichenau, 'can never be too high. They sow the seeds of future greatness.' And the historian Hugh Trevor-Roper said: 'Like an ancient hero, Hitler wished to be sent with human sacrifices to the grave.'

Hitler, although he knew all hope had gone, waited in his bunker until 30 April 1945 before shooting himself, with Eva Braun, whom he had just married. The date was too significant to occultists to be a coincidence. It was the day that ends in Walpurgis night – the high feast of the powers of darkness.

The sum of human knowledge

The ancient art of interpreting numbers answers to a deep-seated human need to find meaning in even the most commonplace things and events. HILDI HAWKINS explains the procedures and theories of the numerologists

The 'Hebrew' numerological system							
1	**2**	**3**	**4**	**5**	**6**	**7**	**8**
A	B	C	D	E	U	O	F
I	K	G	M	H	V	Z	P
Q	R	L	T	N	W		
J		S			X		
Y							

Left: the table most generally used by numerologists to calculate the number corresponding to a particular name or word

Below: a magic square – a number array in which rows, columns and diagonals add up to the same total – is shown behind the gloomy figure in Dürer's engraving *Melencolia I* (1514). Such squares, epitomising the mystical properties of numbers, have often been used as magic talismans

CAN NUMBERS REVEAL the future? Or show the hidden aspects of a person's character? Practitioners of the ancient art of numerology believe they can.

Numerology is a method of making names, dates or events correspond to numbers – generally between one and nine, although sometimes 11 and 22 are included in the system. Each number has a certain significance: William Shakespeare corresponds to five, the number of versatility and resourcefulness.

The correspondence is established by a very simple identification of the letters of the alphabet with numbers according to the 'Hebrew system', as numerologists call it (see table).

To find your number, simply write down the number corresponding to each letter of your name, and add them together. If the resulting number is over nine, add up its digits and keep doing this until the result is less than 10. For instance, the letters of the name Charlotte Brontë add to five. (Charlotte = $3+5+1+2+3+7+4+4+5 = 34$; Brontë $= 2+2+7+5+4+5 = 25$; $34+25 = 59$; $5+9 = 14$; $1+4 = 5$.)

If the digits corresponding to your name add up to one, you are probably a dominant kind of person, a leader. 'Ones' are pioneers, inventors, designers – but they often put their plans into practice with little regard for the way they will affect the people most directly involved. They tend to dominate everyone they meet, they rarely have close friends and are sometimes, despite their confident appearance, very lonely people.

Two is interpreted by modern numerologists as the number of passive, receptive people. 'Twos' are quiet, unambitious, gentle, kind, tidy and conscientious. They often get their own way, however, by gentle persuasion rather than force. They are inclined to be hesitant, to make problems for themselves by putting off decisions for no good reason, and this quality can lead them into difficult situations.

Three is one of the most extrovert numbers, belonging to intelligent, creative and witty people, who generally make friends easily and seem to succeed at anything to which they turn their hands. They are proud, ambitious and pleasure-loving, but their great weakness lies in their inability to take anything – ideas or people – seriously for very long.

Four, like two, is a number corresponding to dependable, down-to-earth people. They are born organisers. They lack the volatility of 'ones' and 'threes', but they make up for this by their fairness and meticulous attention to detail. They may be subject to sudden

People whose names correspond to five are said to be clever and fast-moving, though feckless. Numerologists find confirmation in eminent people as diverse as Shakespeare (left), whom Coleridge called 'our myriad-minded Shakespeare', and Charlotte Brontë (below), who has been described as presenting the condition of women in early 19th-century England with an unprecedented 'frankness and ardour'

Below: the skyline of Manhattan at dusk. New York's number is three – representing pride, ambition and love of pleasure, but an inability to take ideas and people seriously for long. An apt description of the glittering capital of American finance and fashion?

irrational rages or depressions that seem extraordinary in people who are usually models of calmness. Four has traditionally been regarded by numerologists as the number of ill-luck; people whose number is four often seem to pay dearly for any success they achieve in life.

Five is the number of bright, fast-moving, clever, impatient people. They live on their nerves, and love meeting people and seeking out new experiences. They are often physically attractive but rather feckless, hating to be tied down. Five is the number that represents sex (the digits of which also add up to five), and people whose number is five often have varied and exciting love-lives, often problematic. Sometimes the sexual side of their nature shows itself in excesses or perversions.

People whose number is six are among the happiest of the whole numerological system. They are happy, tranquil, well-balanced and home-loving. They are affectionate, loyal, sincere and conscientious. They are not uncreative; many of them are successful in the performing arts. The negative aspect of their character is their tendency to be rather fussy, conceited and self-satisfied.

Seven is the number of the loner, the introspective scholar, philosopher, mystic or occultist. These people tend to stand aside from the mainstream of life, content to observe it. They are dignified, self-controlled and reserved. They tend to be indifferent to worldly wealth but, while they may seem aloof and stand-offish, make loyal friends. Despite their powerful intellects, they are often surprisingly bad at putting their thoughts into words, and may even dislike discussing them if they feel their ideas are being challenged.

Eight represents worldly success, and people who have this number often make successful businessmen, politicians or lawyers. Their success is, however, often built on a great deal of hard work, which is often done at considerable expense to their warmer, more human qualities. They often seem to be hard, egocentric and grasping; but there can be, behind the unsympathetic exterior, a whimsical streak that endears them to other people.

Nine stands for the height of intellectual and spiritual achievement. People whose number is nine are the idealists, the romantics, the visionaries – poets, missionaries, doctors, religious teachers, brilliant scientists. Their great qualities are their unselfishness, their self-discipline and their determination. Their idealism is concerned with mankind as a whole – in their everyday lives they may be inclined to seek the limelight,

Above: King's College, Cambridge. Seven is the number of the city – and of philosophers and scholars

Eleven is the number of those with a strong sense of vocation – from leaders such as Churchill (left) to reformers such as Florence Nightingale (far left). Human relationships mean less to them than their ideas: Einstein (below left) called himself a 'lone traveller'. What Picasso (below) was told by his mother could be said of any of them: 'If you become a soldier you'll be a general. If you become a monk you'll end up as the Pope'

and to be fickle friends or lovers.

Some numerologists also employ the numbers 11 and 22. They believe that these numbers represent a higher plane of experience than the numbers one to nine. Eleven is the number of those who experience revelations and suffer martyrdom; those with names that add up to this number are often people with a strong vocation for their work – preachers, doctors, nurses or teachers. They tend to prefer ideas to real people.

Twenty-two is the 'master' number: people whose names add to 22 combine the best qualities of all the other numbers.

Apply this procedure to the name you were given at birth and you will find, numerologists claim, the characteristics you were born with and that will underlie your personality throughout your life; apply it to the name you apply to yourself, or would like to have, and you will discover how your experiences in the world have moulded your

regarded as indicating a general type, not a detailed description. But that people whose names add to the same number share certain personality traits can be supported with numerous examples: the letters of the names Winston S. Churchill, Einstein, Pablo Picasso and Florence Nightingale, for instance, all add to 11 – the number of those with strong vocations.

The same technique can be applied to the names of cities, and many of the results seem to confirm the beliefs of numerologists. London adds up to five, indicating many-sidedness and resilience; New York to three, indicating brilliance and glitter. The ancient cities of Oxford and Cambridge both have the number seven – the number of the aloof, inward-turned scholar.

But the ridiculous extremes to which numerology can be taken are indicated by the prediction of an American numerologist that, since Oakland, California, shares the number nine with Chicago, it will one day suffer a great fire, as did Chicago in 1871.

Numerology extends to the character of a year, a decade or a century. The present century carries the number one $(1+9+0+0 = 10; 1+0 = 1)$ and, according to numerologists, should be an ebullient time of invention and discovery, dominance and subjugation. All of this could be said to be true, although (here lies the weakness of the loose collection of attributes associated with each number) it could be regarded as equally true of the 19th century.

The year 1979 was characterised by the number eight $(1+9+7+9 = 26; 2+6 = 8)$. According to numerologists, it should have been a year when financial and political matters went exceptionally well. The 1980s are the ninth decade and should be characterised by nine, with great achievements in the arts and the world of learning.

Past decades are depicted by numerologists as confirming their theories: the brilliant 1920s, a 3-decade, followed by the more subdued 1930s, overshadowed in its latter half by the threat of war; the recovery of confidence of the 1940s and the self-assurance of the 6-decade of the 1950s; the

personality. Using a nickname, you will be able to ascertain what your friends think of you. Comparing her maiden and married names, a married woman can find out how married life has changed her.

The total of vowel numbers in your name is your heart number, which shows your inner character; the total of consonants is your personality number, which indicates your outward personality, or the impression you make on the people around you. (This distinction is derived from Hebrew, in which only the consonants of any word are actually written down; the vowels are therefore 'hidden', and represent the aspects of the personality that are not outwardly apparent.)

Like the character types suggested by the sign of the zodiac you were born under, the traits indicated by these numbers are to be

The 1920s (top), the third decade of the century, had the number three – the number of the pleasure-loving and fickle. The 1930s (centre) corresponded to four, representing unstable moods and ill-luck; the decade began with the Depression (a Christmas Day dole queue is shown here) and ended with the Second World War. After VE Day (above), the 1940s saw the return of prosperity and renewed experiment in fashions and life-styles – in character with the decade's number, five ('bright, clever, impatient')

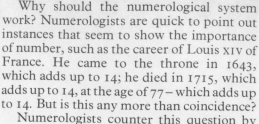

Why should the numerological system work? Numerologists are quick to point out instances that seem to show the importance of number, such as the career of Louis XIV of France. He came to the throne in 1643, which adds up to 14; he died in 1715, which adds up to 14, at the age of 77 – which adds up to 14. But is this any more than coincidence?

Numerologists counter this question by claiming that there is no such thing as coincidence. They believe the Universe is like a vast harp with countless strings, each vibrating at a certain rate, characterised by a number. Number, they believe, is at the root of all things and they point out that science

dreaming withdrawal into mysticism of the 1960s, characterised by the number seven, and the hardening up of attitudes in the money-conscious 1970s, reflected in its number, eight. But this appropriateness is in the eye of the beholder: for example, some might view the 1950s, which saw the appearance of the H-bomb and rock'n'roll, and the intensification of the cold war, as badly represented by six (happy, tranquil, balanced).

Numerologists believe that numbers can be used to suggest beneficial courses of action. If your number is seven, for example, you should take care to make difficult decisions or perform important tasks on days of the month that add up to seven: the seventh, the 16th and the 25th. People whose names add up to eight should eat plenty of oranges, since the word 'oranges' adds up to eight – but presumably never a single orange at a time! Certain years, too, can be good or bad for an individual; to find your year-number, add your month and date of birth to the *current* year: 1981, for instance, is a 9-year for someone born on 24 February 1956 ($24 + 2 + 1981 = 2007$; $2 + 0 + 0 + 7 = 9$), indicating it is a year of high spiritual and intellectual achievement.

The 1950s (top) seem poorly characterised by their number, six (happy and well-balanced). But seven (the mystic and occult) seems appropriate to the 1960s, the hippy decade (above). And eight, the number of businessmen, politicians and lawyers, seems to suit the 1970s, the decade of oil crises (below)

has found that light, sound, atomic structure and many other things are dependent on frequency, or number. But what of the objection that, even if this view of the Universe is correct, basing the system on a person's name must be wrong, since the naming of a child is largely a matter of the personal tastes and whims of the parents? The numerologists have their answers ready; as Florence Campbell, an American, explains:

> The Soul has taken many journeys in the past and *knows* its present needs. The Soul wants progress upwards on the Great Spiral and *chooses* for the incarnating ego the vowels whose total shall accomplish this purpose. . . . There is a long 'Dark Cycle' before the child is born, and during this Dark Cycle the vibrations that are to label the new life are so impressed upon the subconscious minds of the parents that they are compelled to carry out the plan.

In other words, the numerologist believes that the name each person carries is no accident, and that it tells something significant about its bearer, in a code to which the numerologist has the key.

Ancient philosophers were enthralled by the mathematical relationships they found in nature, and believed that numbers underlay every aspect of reality. This chapter explains how certain numbers then acquired their own symbolic 'personality'

THE MOST FUNDAMENTAL arithmetical operation is tallying: the matching, one for one, of one set of objects with another – or with marks in the dust, or pebbles, or knots in a string – in order to compare quantities. The next step is to give names to numbers and to match objects against *these* in sequence – that is, to count. Some peoples, such as certain New Guineans and Brazilian Indians, have no names for numbers beyond three. And the number words that do exist may vary according to the type of object being counted. (This survives in modern English: we speak of a brace of gamebirds, pistols or dogs, but of nothing else.) It must have been a magical moment when the abstract nature of number was realised: the idea that three trees, three people, or even a collection of three different things all had one thing in common: their 'threeness'.

The power of this abstract idea must have been apparent very early. Number seemed

The thought that counts

Above: the Beast from the sea described in chapter 13 of the book of Revelation, as portrayed in a German altarpiece of about 1400. The meaning of the Beast's 7 heads, 10 horns and 10 crowns, and of its number, 666, has been the subject of much speculation by number mystics. They have variously interpreted the Beast as representing Rome, the emperor Nero, and even Napoleon Bonaparte

Left: Pythagoras and a disciple experiment with musical tones. The size of a bell or the amount of water in a cup determines the pitch of the note each produces. The discovery by Pythagoras that simple numerical ratios between these quantities correspond to harmony or discord between notes fed his belief that 'all is number'

somehow to underlie reality: all collections of three objects were united by their 'three-ness'. At a very deep level, perhaps they were the *same*. It is small wonder that the mysterious power of the concept of number inspired a powerful tradition of mystical thought that still colours the way we think about numbers. The tradition comes to us from the medieval Christian Church, which in turn drew its inspiration from two major intellectual traditions, Greek Pythagoreanism and Hebrew *gematria*.

The school of Pythagoras was a religious community founded by the semi-legendary figure of Pythagoras in the Greek colony of Croton, in southern Italy, around 530 BC. It was dedicated to the study of geometry, mathematics and astronomy, and to experimentation in music. The Pythagorean school studied the variations in pitch produced by vibrating strings of varying lengths, and is credited with the discovery that musical intervals may be represented in terms of simple ratios of whole numbers.

It may have been the discovery of the mathematical nature of musical intervals that gave the Pythagoreans their idea that number was the key to the Universe. Whatever the origin of the belief, they clung to it fervently and bequeathed it to the West.

Like all Greeks, they thought of number geometrically. One was a point, two a line, three a triangle, the first plane figure, and four a tetrahedron (which resembles a pyramid, but has a triangular base), the first solid figure. These four numbers between them thus describe the whole of space. The Pythagoreans venerated them in a symmetrical pattern called the *tetractys*, and believed it was 'eternal nature's fountain spring'.

Number pervaded the Pythagoreans' entire cosmology. Creation was seen as the division of primordial unity into parts. Each number had a certain significance attached to it; broadly, the Pythagoreans believed that the world was composed of a series of ten pairs of opposites corresponding to oddness or evenness in numbers – limited/unlimited, right/left, male/female, and so on.

In Hebrew, as in Greek, numbers were represented by letters of the alphabet, and this may well have stimulated *gematria*, the Jewish art of turning names into numbers. This was done simply by totalling the numbers that the letters stood for. The central idea of *gematria* was that things referred to by words whose letters added up to the same number were somehow the same; number expressed their true essence.

This technique was applied, for example, to the story told in Genesis 18: Abraham was sitting at the door of his tent in the plains of Mamre 'and lo, three men stood by him'. The Hebrew for 'and lo, three men' adds, by *gematria*, to 701 – and so do the words 'these are Michael, Gabriel and Raphael'. The obvious conclusion was that the three 'men' were actually archangels.

It was natural for early Christians to take up the numerological ideas of the two dominant intellectual traditions – Greek and Jewish – that surrounded them. The early symbol of the dove for Christ, for example, was probably adopted because the Greek letters alpha and omega – 'I am Alpha and Omega, the beginning and the ending, saith the Lord' (Revelation 1:8) – add to 801, the number of *peristera*, the Greek for 'dove'.

For the Christians, as for the Pythagoreans, goodness and maleness were associated with the odd numbers. One stands

Top: to the Greeks, the number one corresponded to a point, and two to a line; three points defined a triangle, the simplest plane figure; four points defined a tetrahedron, the simplest space-occupying form. The Pythagorean *tetractys* (above) was composed of one, two, three and four dots arranged in rows

Below: in Hebrew, numbers are represented by letters. To write 456 the letters for 400, 50 and 6 would be written together

for perfection, unity, God. Two, as the first number to break away from that perfection, represents the Devil. And since odd numbers dominate in addition (odd + even = odd), and addition represents sexual union, odd numbers must represent the male sex.

The Bible, early Christian theologians believed, provided confirmation of the evil associated with two. For in the account of the Creation, did not God neglect on the second day to find that his work was good? And before the Flood, the unclean animals went into Noah's ark two by two, whereas the clean animals went in by sevens.

Modern numerologists are more generous to the number two, preferring to emphasise its positive qualities, but it nonetheless remains the least favoured of the numbers (see page 66).

Three is the first male number. One by itself, although perfect, is barren; two introduces a discord that can only be resolved by adding the two numbers together to make three. It is this symbolism that is behind the Christian doctrine of the Trinity; as the 19th-century French magician Eliphas Levi put it:

Were God only one, He would never be creator or father. Were He two, there would be antagonism or division in the infinite, which would mean the division also, or death, of all possible things. He is therefore three for the creation by Himself and in His image of the infinite multitude of beings and numbers.

The number of ill-luck

Four is the Pythagorean number of solid earth, being the number of points required to define a tetrahedron. It may be solid and uninspiring, but as Plutarch put it, writing around the turn of the first century AD, 'Those who exalt Four teach us a lesson that is not without value, that by reason of this number all solids came into being.' But four is also the number of evil and ill-luck, being made up of two twos, in two different ways ($4 = 2 + 2 = 2 \times 2$).

Five, on the other hand, is the number of male sexuality: it is made up of two and three: the first feminine number added to the first masculine number. Thus, in love, woman is given to man – and man 'naturally' dominates.

Six is the first 'perfect' number – it is the sum of its factors (numbers that divide it without remainder). Thus $6 = 1 + 2 + 3$. Perfect numbers were venerated for their tranquillity and harmoniousness. In ancient times only the first four perfect numbers were known: 6, 28, 496 and 8128. The next one – 33,550,336 – was apparently not discovered until the mid 15th century.

Seven is a number rich in biblical associations. There are seven deadly sins, seven Christian virtues, seven petitions in the Lord's prayer; on the seventh day of the siege of Jericho, Joshua marched seven times

Hebrew numerals

1	2	3	4	5	6	7	8	9
א	ב	ג	ד	ה	ו	ז	ח	ט
10	**20**	**30**	**40**	**50**	**60**	**70**	**80**	**90**
י	כ	ל	מ	נ	ס	ע	פ	צ
100	**200**	**300**	**400**	**500**	**600**	**700**	**800**	**900**
ק	ר	ש	ת	ך	ם	ן	ף	ץ

One of the more eccentric manifestations of mankind's fascination with number symbolism is pyramidology. One pyramidologist in particular, an American named Worth Smith, claimed that the Grand Gallery of the Great Pyramid of Cheops (right) enshrined a complete history of the Christian Church, with particular emphasis on Britain's history. (He believed the pyramid was built by ancestors of the British.)

He believed that the point at which the Grand Gallery begins represents Christ's birth on 6 October in the year 4 BC. Each inch (2.5 centimetres) represents a year. For the first 400 inches (10 metres) the stones are smooth; then they suddenly become scarred and broken. This, Smith claimed, represented the first 400 years of the Church's existence, a reasonably peaceful period that ended with the invasion by the Visigoths.

The prophetic insight of the Egyptian builders – or their lack of engineering

Pyramids and prophecies

skill – is demonstrated by another badly surfaced stretch: this, according to Smith, represents the rise of Islam from 622 (Mohammed's flight from Mecca) to an important defeat in Europe in 732.

At the point supposedly corresponding to 1844 the gallery ends in the Great Step, which is 3 feet (1 metre) high. This should represent some kind of improvement in the fortunes of Christendom, but Smith is forced to admit that there was no great advance in 1844. He theorises rather lamely that 'almost the whole lot of the discoveries and inventions in common usage have come into existence since the year 1844.'

According to Smith the scale now changes so that one inch represents a month. A new tunnel, the Low Passage, supposedly begins on 4 August 1914, the date of Britain's entry into the First World War, and ends on 9 November, date of the Kaiser's abdication. Smith expected the current year – 1936 – to see the dethronement of Satan himself.

Right: the Devil tempts Jesus, in a 12th-century painting from the ceiling of a Swiss church. The time that Jesus spent in the wilderness being tempted by the Devil was 40 days and 40 nights – a period that occurs often in the myth and folklore of all countries

Left: the Trinity, painted by El Greco in about 1600. God the Father cradles Jesus, his son, while the Holy Spirit, in the form of a dove, hovers above. The difficult notion of the three-in-one God is not explicitly stated in the Bible, but was formulated by theologians to reconcile various conceptions of God scattered through the Old and New Testaments. To numerologists, God could not be single, since he would then be uncreative; nor twofold, since this is the nature of antagonism and conflict

round the walls of the city and flattened them with a blast from seven trumpets; and Pharaoh's dream, which Joseph interpreted, involved seven fat and seven lean cows, seven plump ears of corn and seven blighted ones. In folklore, too, mystery attaches to the number seven; magical properties are attributed to seventh sons and seventh sons of seventh sons. The power of the number seven stretches far back in time: around 2500 BC the great Sumerian king Lugulan-nemund built a temple in the city of Adab to the goddess Nintu, with seven gates and seven doors, purified with the sacrifice of seven times seven fatted oxen and sheep. One can only guess at the significance of this frequent use of the number – but it seems that it is linked with the phases of the Moon, which take about $28 (= 4 \times 7)$ days to go through a complete cycle. The ancients believed that the cycles of birth and death, growth and decay, depend on the waxing and waning of the Moon.

The symbolism of the numbers eight and

nine is connected with human procreation: a woman's body has eight orifices, the eighth being the one through which new life enters the world. Eight is thus the number of worldly success. Nine is the number of completeness because a human child is conceived, formed and born in nine months.

A few numbers greater than nine were regarded as having a special significance. Twelve, for instance, is a number of completeness: there are 12 months in the year, 12 signs of the zodiac, 12 tribes of Israel and, of course, 12 disciples. Thirteen is a number of excess – it goes one beyond a number of completeness. The fact that there were 13 people at the Last Supper strengthens the uneasiness many people still feel about the number. This feeling is so strong that, for instance, when Queen Elizabeth II visited West Germany in 1965, the number of the platform at Duisburg station from which her train left was changed from 13 to 12a.

One more number with ancient sacred and mystical connections is 40. The rain that caused the Flood in Genesis continued for 40 days and 40 nights; this is also the time that

Below: 13 people are present at the Last Supper: Jesus and the 12 disciples, of whom one, Judas Iscariot, turns away in shame. This scene, familiar to all Christians, strengthened the superstitions that surrounded the number 13

Bottom: 'The Great Beast' is the inscription in Greek on the medallion worn by the magician Aleister Crowley in this self-portrait. Crowley adopted the mysterious number ascribed to the Beast in the book of Revelation: 'six hundred threescore and six'

Moses spent on Mount Sinai, speaking with God. The children of Israel walked 40 years in the wilderness, and Jesus was tempted by the Devil for 40 days and 40 nights. Forty has been sacred since ancient Babylonian times, when it was known as *kissatum*, 'the excellent quality'. The Greek poet Hesiod, writing in the eighth century BC, explains that 40 days is the period for which the star cluster called the Pleiades disappears. These stars are of widespread importance: ancient authors state that autumn sowing should be performed when the Pleiades set at dawn, and some peoples use them to mark the passage of a year. The 40-day disappearance of the Pleiades may also have started the habit of measuring periods of time of agricultural significance in 40-day periods – as in the belief that a fine St Swithin's day (15 July) will be followed by 40 days of good weather, while a rainy one presages 40 days of rain.

Armed with these interpretations of numbers, the Christian theologian had at his fingertips a powerful tool for unravelling the

hidden meaning of any biblical text. The crowning glory of biblical number symbolism is the book of Revelation. Written in 22 chapters – the 'master' number, the number of things traditionally supposed to have been created by God, the number of letters in the Hebrew alphabet – it is full of numerological puzzles. The greatest and most famous of these is the puzzle of the number of the Beast, 666:

And I stood upon the sand of the sea, and saw a beast rise up out of the sea, having seven heads and ten horns, and upon his horns ten crowns, and upon his heads the name of blasphemy. . . . And I saw one of his heads as it were wounded to death; and his deadly wound was healed: and all the world wondered after the beast. . . . Let him that hath understanding count the number of the beast: for it is the number of a man; and his number is Six hundred threescore and six.

The identity of the Beast

There have been many conjectures as to the identity of the Beast. It is now generally accepted that the Beast is meant to stand for the Roman empire, and the seven heads for seven emperors. The head wounded to death and then healed could represent Nero; he was murdered in AD 68, but there were persistent rumours that he lived on. Nero, in Hebrew, adds up to 666 – but only if spelt with an extra N. Otherwise it adds up to 616 – and some early manuscripts do, indeed, give the number of the Beast as 616. The 'image of the Beast' of chapter 15 may represent Caligula, who in AD 30 had set up a statue of himself in the Holy of Holies in Jerusalem, and gave the order that the Jews were to worship it (although he died before the command could be enforced). Gaius Caligula Caesar in Hebrew adds to 616, as does Gaios Kaisar in Greek.

Numerologists, however, have not been content with these simple explanations, and speculations as to the Beast's identity have ranged far and wide. In the early 19th century there was an attempt to make Napoleon into the Beast. Thomas Macaulay, the English statesman, refused to accept this hypothesis; with typically mordant wit, he announced that the House of Commons was obviously the Beast: it had 658 members, three clerks, a serjeant and a deputy, a doorkeeper, a chaplain and a librarian – making 666 in all. The magician Aleister Crowley believed *himself* to be the Beast; he had, he claimed, discovered his true identity while still a boy, with 'a passionately ecstatic sense of identity'. He signed himself 'The Beast 666' – or sometimes *To mega therion*, which means 'the great Beast' in Greek. Its number is 666.

Numbered among the great

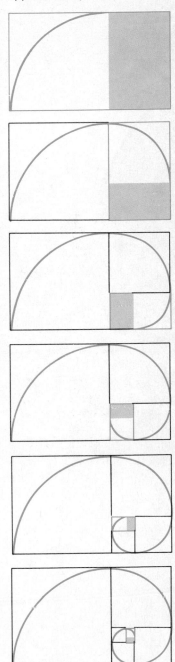

Number lies behind scientific theory, ideas of artistic proportion and rules of musical harmony. Many great thinkers have been convinced that number is therefore the very essence of the world. This chapter explains how artists and scientists have seen meaning in number, and how patterns of numbers have guided them in their creative work

THE BELIEF THAT NUMBER is the key to the secrets of the Universe – a belief verging on the mystical – lay at the heart of many arts and branches of learning up to, and even after, the scientific revolution of the 17th century. It was the inspiration for some of their most spectacular achievements. Diverse disciplines were brought together by the common language of number: music, astronomy, architecture, poetry and theology reflected the *harmonia mundi*, the harmony of the world, by means of number.

Number was in everything; a typical expression of this idea is St Augustine's remark on dancing:

Ask what delights you in dancing and number will reply, 'Lo, here am I!' Examine the beauty of bodily form, and you will find that everything is in its place by number. Examine the beauty of bodily motion, and you will

find everything in its due time by number.

Number was the essence of the *harmonia mundi*. And so the way to create a perfect work of art was to use number in the correct way. This belief can be traced to Plato, who states in his philosophical dialogue *Philebus*: 'The qualities of measure and proportion invariably . . . constitute beauty and elegance.' The architect Leon Battista Alberti, writing in the mid 15th century, echoes the idea:

Nature is sure to act consistently, and with a constant Analogy in all her operations: from whence I conclude, that the same Numbers, by means of which the Agreement of Sounds affects our ears with delight, are the very same which please our eyes and minds.

The large number of handbooks on architectural proportion that appeared during the Renaissance are testimony to the seriousness with which this idea was regarded. And in the 20th century a major attempt at constructing a harmonious system of design by proportion was made by the great architect Le Corbusier.

Golden proportions

Called the Modulor, Corbusier's system was based on the golden section, a ratio regarded since ancient times as especially pleasing. If a line is divided into unequal parts in such a way that the ratio of the whole to the longer part equals the ratio of the longer part to the shorter, the line is said to be divided in golden section. This ratio is called by the Greek letter 'phi'. It is approximately equal to 1.618. If this number is repeatedly multiplied by itself, a series of numbers is formed, every member of which (after the first two) is equal to the sum of the proceding two numbers.

A simpler example of such a series – they are called Fibonacci series after Leonardo Fibonacci, a mathematician who worked in Pisa about 1200 – is the sequence: 1, 2, 3, 5, 8.... Fibonacci series are found in the proportions and ratios of many natural patterns: the pads on a cat's foot, the arrangement of leaves on a plant, the spirals of a snail's shell.

Building by numbers

Corbusier claimed that the proportions of ideal human figures embodied the golden section, and that buildings designed in accordance with it would be both beautiful and well-adapted to human needs. He designed several buildings using the Fibonacci series, based on the figure of a man 6 feet (1.8 metres) tall. He even believed that his system had reconciled the metric and imperial systems of units. The buildings based on the Modulor include the chapel at Ronchamp, in France, blocks of flats in many famous cities, and the administrative centre at Chandigarh, in the Punjab.

Are these buildings more beautiful than others not constructed on any particular system of proportion? The question is almost impossible to answer, since the buildings named are the work of a great architect and, as such, are likely to be better than those of an indifferent architect, whether designed according to a system or not.

It is even doubtful that the golden section leads to more beautiful proportions than any other ratio. A rectangle with length and breadth in the ratio of the golden section has long been regarded as in some sense ideal. Yet as long ago as 1876 it was found by experiment that, although subjects preferred golden-section rectangles in the laboratory (35 per cent chose them when offered a choice of 10 rectangles), a much shorter rectangle was preferred for pictures in a

The golden section, which fascinated Le Corbusier, occurs repeatedly in the windows and recesses of his chapel at Ronchamp (above). His Modulor system was based on a man 6 feet (183 centimetres) tall. In the 'red' series this height is divided in golden section by the height of the navel. The 'blue' series is based on the height of the raised hand, above the ground and above the groin. Dividing these distances (shown here in centimetres) by the golden section extends the two series (right), which are related to basic human postures (below)

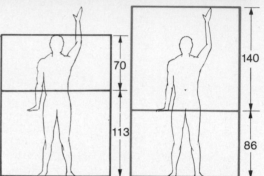

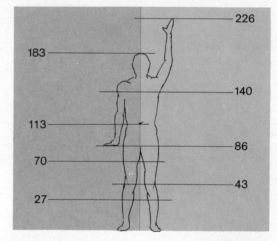

Le Corbusier believed that the dimensions of his Modulor series were as convenient to use in imperial units as in metric	
centimetres	inches
226	89
183	72
140	55
113	44½
86	34
70	27½
43	17
27	10½

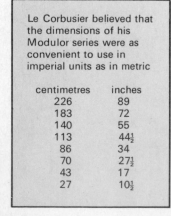

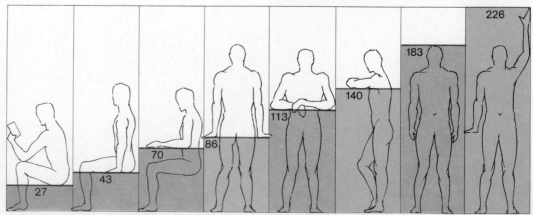

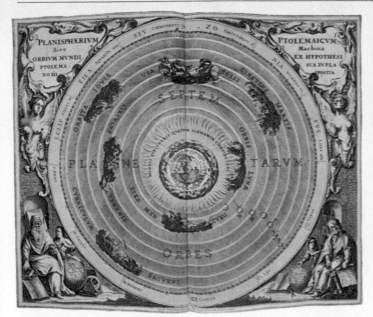

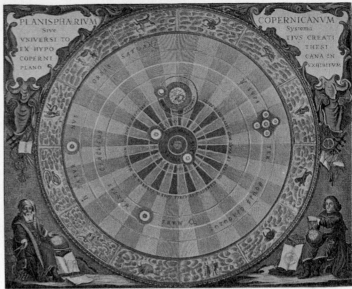

gallery – 5:4 for upright shapes, 4:3 for horizontal. If it were the case that certain proportions were preferred, then, as the architectural writer P. H. Scholfield points out:

> One would expect the same types of relationships to have appeared spontaneously in all periods of good design.
> In fact, this is not the case, and the sorts of mathematical relationships which occur are closely related to the mathematical knowledge of the period.

What role is played by number relationships in science? The idea that there was an underlying numerical harmony in the world made it natural for the ancients to seek scientific explanations in terms of number. Reasoning of this sort led them to think that God must have made the world in six days because six is the first 'perfect' number – a number equal to the sum of its factors (see page 71).

Today it seems that such an argument has no validity whatever. Yet it is undeniable that important discoveries have been made when numerical patterns have been noticed in natural phenomena, even if explanations for those patterns were still unknown.

An example is the Titius-Bode 'law', which led to the discovery of the asteroids. It was noticed that the relative distances of the planets from the Sun fall roughly into a sequence of numbers generated by a simple mathematical rule. But there is a gap in the series, between Mars and Jupiter. It was argued that there should be a planet at the corresponding position. A search was made, and an object was indeed found there. It was not a planet but the first known asteroid – a small rocky body, one of thousands that are now known.

Another example of scientific discovery guided by numerical patterns comes from chemistry. In the 19th century the Russian chemist Dmitri Mendeleev noticed that when the elements are listed in order of their

Above: the transition from an Earth-centred view of the Universe (left) to a Sun-centred view (right) was made largely on grounds of mathematical elegance and harmony. The ancient system worked well (despite the dejected appearance of the ancient astronomers depicted at the foot of this map, drawn in 1660). Yet many of the most able scientists accepted the arguments of Copernicus for the mathematically simpler Sun-centred system, even before telescopic evidence supported the theory

Below: Dmitri Mendeleev, the Russian chemist whose classification of the elements on the basis of their atomic weights underlies modern chemistry

atomic weights (which are, literally, the relative weights of their atoms), patterns emerge: the list can be arranged in rows and columns so that the chemical properties change systematically along the rows and down the columns. To make this system work, it was sometimes necessary to revise the atomic weights assigned to certain elements, or to suppose that there were gaps, corresponding to as yet undiscovered elements. Subsequent discoveries vindicated Mendeleev's ideas triumphantly. All known elements fit neatly into this 'periodic' table, and modern knowledge of atomic structure explains why these patterns should exist.

The modern view

The modern attitude to such numerical relationships among phenomena, empirically found, is very different from that which was prevalent as late as the 18th century. We see them as the inevitable product of relatively simple physical laws: ancient philosophers and scientists, not knowing their explanations, saw every such instance of regularity as another proof of the harmonious and beautiful design of the world.

The desire to see the world as a place ruled by harmony and governed by number may seem naïve today, but it is an expression of the perennial tendency – and desire – of human beings to see order and pattern in everything around them. Number may not be everything, but the unprovable assumption that nature is rational and intelligible is the basis of science – and of the practical reasoning of everyday life.

A radical attempt to account for this intelligibility of the Universe was made by the German philosopher Immanuel Kant in the 18th century. He saw the source of the orderliness of the world as being the human mind itself, and the concepts with which it does its thinking. He went so far as to say: 'Our intellect does not draw its laws from nature . . . but imposes them on nature.'

Cause and effect, time and space, the laws of mathematics and logic, are the result of the constitution of our minds.

Sir Arthur Eddington, an English astronomer, pushed a form of this idea even further in the early 20th century. He believed that many highly detailed facts about the Universe – namely, the value of certain numerical constants – could be calculated without any appeal to experiment or observation, but by pure mathematics alone.

But very few scientists and philosophers have accepted this view. The specific features of the Universe are not to be explained by reference to the structure of the human mind: and only experience can show which theories are actually true of the world. It is therefore highly remarkable that the Universe should prove to obey laws that are in fact simple, and harmonious.

Even more remarkable: nature has (so far) proved to be not only intelligible by rational laws but intelligible in a way that is frequently elegant and even beautiful. When Copernicus put forward his idea that the Earth revolved around the Sun, rather than vice versa, it was not so much the experimental evidence as the theory's elegance, or aesthetic appeal, that was persuasive to contemporary thinkers.

Similarly, Einstein developed the theory of relativity on the premise that 'absolute' motion does not exist; that is, there can be no justification for saying that, of two scientific observers moving relatively to each other, one is 'really' at rest and the other is not. There is no absolute standard of rest in the

Above: Immanuel Kant believed the mathematical regularities of the world to be, in some sense, created by the human mind

Universe. Einstein was very little influenced by the problems raised by such experiments as that of American physicists Michelson and Morley. The grace and inherent power of the theory played a large part in the theory's quick acceptance and the conviction of scientists that it *must* be true.

That the laws of nature should be not only rational but elegant seems almost too much to expect. Yet this astonishing metaphysical hypothesis is constantly being borne out by science. Time and again physical reality is found to coincide with the speculations of scientists, evolved from a few basic facts and couched in the subtle language of mathematics. The existence of many subatomic particles has been suggested by 'gaps' in mathematical patterns somewhat analogous to Mendeleev's table of the elements. The branch of mathematics responsible for these achievements, called 'group theory', was evolved between the World Wars as a part of purely abstract algebra; yet it seemed tailormade for the understanding of particles that were to be discovered decades later.

In view of these amazing anticipations of experimental results by the mathematical speculations of theoretical physicists, how does modern science differ from numerology? It differs in that it makes no assumptions about the symbolic meaning of numbers: numbers do not give insight into some divine master plan of the Universe. But the assumption on which science rests – that nature is regular and comprehensible by human reason – is every bit as mystical as the idea that 'number is all'.

Music of the spheres

The work of the great astronomer Johannes Kepler (1571–1630) shows a curious fusion of numerological and scientific thought. It was Kepler who formulated the extraordinarily elegant laws that govern planetary motion. This man,

one of the first great modern scientists, was also a profound mystic.

Like Pythagoras and Plato, Kepler believed that the world was ruled by number. He tried hard to prove that the distances of the planets from the Sun were given by an arrangement of Euclid's five regular solids (left); by doing so, he believed, he could demonstrate something of the order of the mind of God. But his faith in number went further: he believed that musical harmony, mathematically expressed, and the harmony of the spheres were one and the same thing: 'I affirm and demonstrate that the movements [of the planets] are modulated according to harmonic proportions.'

Kepler could not resist pushing his theory further. Each planet, he believed, sings a characteristic tune – and, by a calculation involving the angle it describes in a day, as seen from the Sun, he was able to work out what the tune for each planet was. The Earth sings a simple little ditty – mi fa mi – indicating, Kepler asserted, that 'in this our domicile *mi*sery and *fa*mine obtain.'

The search for the Philosopher's Stone

The dream of finding a substance that could transform base metals into gold has lured alchemists for thousands of years. Although now generally derided as no more than misguided mystics, these passionate researchers actually contributed much to scientific knowledge. And some reliable witnesses have claimed that, for a select few alchemists, the dream came true. BRIAN INNES narrates the history of this ancient occult science

crumb as big as a rape or turnip seed, saying, receive this small parcel of the greatest treasure of the world, which truly few kings or princes have ever known or seen.'

Most ungratefully, Schweitzer protested that this was not sufficient to transmute as much as four grains of lead into gold; whereupon the stranger took it back, cut it in half, and flung one part in the fire, exclaiming: 'It is yet sufficient for thee!'

Schweitzer then confessed his former theft, and described his lack of success. The stranger laughed and said:

Thou art more dextrous to commit theft than to apply thy medicine; for if thou hadst only wrapped up thy stolen prey in yellow wax, to preserve it from the arising fumes of lead, it would have penetrated to the bottom of the lead, and transmuted it to gold.

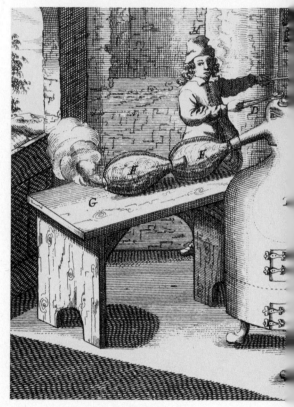

TWO DAYS AFTER CHRISTMAS in 1666, an unprepossessing stranger visited Johann Friedrich Schweitzer, physician to the Prince of Orange. He was

of a mean stature, a little long face, with a few small pock holes, and most black hair, not at all curled, a beardless chin, about three or four and forty years of age (as I guessed), and born in North Holland.

It is clear that Schweitzer – the author of one or two books on medical and botanical matters – was a careful and objective observer.

After some idle conversation, the stranger asked Schweitzer whether he would recognise the 'Philosopher's Stone' if he saw it. This was an astounding question. The Philosopher's Stone was the goal of the alchemists – a fabled substance that could transmute metals into gold, banish all illness and bestow long and vigorous life.

The visitor produced from his pocket a small ivory box that held 'three ponderous pieces or small lumps . . . each about the bigness of a small walnut, transparent, of a pale brimstone colour'. This, he said, was the substance that men had sought so long. Schweitzer took one of the pieces greedily, and begged the man to give him just a small piece. When he was refused, he contrived to scrape a speck beneath his fingernail.

When the visitor had left, promising to return in three weeks and show him 'some curious arts in the fire', Schweitzer hurried to his laboratory for a crucible. He melted some lead in it, and then added the tiny piece of stone. But the metal did not change into gold: 'Almost the whole mass of lead flew away, and the remainder turned into a mere glassy earth.'

Impatiently, the physician awaited the return of the stranger, half believing that he would not come again; but in exactly three weeks his mysterious visitor was once more at the door. For a long time the stranger refused to let Schweitzer take another look at the marvellous stone, but at last 'he gave me a

Above: carrying out their investigations blindly, with little understanding of scientific method or the design of experiments, the alchemists nevertheless laid the basis of modern chemical research. Although the alchemical laboratory frequently looked more like a blacksmith's forge, as in this satirical woodcut, the more sophisticated apparatus changed hardly at all in a thousand years

Previous page: the moment at which the First Matter distils over into the receiving flask is caught wonderfully in this painting by the 18th-century artist Joseph Wright of Derby

He promised to return at nine the next morning and show Schweitzer the correct method.

But the next day he came not, nor ever since. Only he sent an excuse at half an hour past nine that morning, by reason of his great business, and promised to come at three in the afternoon, but never came, nor have I heard of him since; whereupon I began to doubt of the whole matter. Nevertheless late that night my wife . . . came soliciting and vexing me to make experiment . . . saying to me, unless this be done, I shall have no rest nor sleep all this night. . . . She being so earnest, I commanded a fire to be made – thinking, alas, now is this man (though so divine in discourse) found guilty of falsehood. . . . My wife wrapped the said matter in wax, and I cut half an ounce or six drams of old lead, and put [it] into a crucible in the fire, which being melted, my wife put in the said Medicine made up in a small pill or button, which presently made such a hissing and bubbling in its perfect operation, that within a quarter of an hour all the mass of lead was transmuted into the . . . finest gold . . . .

The philosopher Spinoza, who lived not far away, came the next day to examine the gold, and was convinced that Schweitzer was telling the truth. The Assay Master of the province, a certain Mr Porelius, tested the metal and pronounced it genuine; and Mr Buectel, the silversmith, subjected it to further tests that confirmed that it was gold.

There is nothing in Schweitzer's account itself to inspire doubt; he was a reputable medical man and a trained scientific observer, and not given to fraud or practical jokes. And yet, knowing what we do now about the nature of matter, and in particular about the properties of metals, it is impossible to believe that such a transmutation could have taken place.

Schweitzer was certainly not the only scientist, however, to be convinced by practical demonstration that the Philosopher's Stone truly existed, and that it would effect the transmutation of base metals into gold. Another was Jan Baptista van Helmont, a respected chemical experimenter. He had been responsible for a number of important discoveries and was the first man to realise that there were other gases than air; indeed, the word 'gas' was his invention. He had written, some 20 years before Schweitzer's meeting with the mysterious stranger:

For truly I have divers times seen it [the Philosopher's Stone] and handled it with my hands, but it was of colour, such as is in Saffron in its powder, yet weighty, and shining like unto powdered glass. There was once given unto me one fourth part of one grain [16 milligrams]. . . . I projected [it] upon eight ounces [227 grams] of quicksilver [mercury] made hot in a crucible; and straightaway all the quicksilver, with a certain degree of noise, stood still from flowing, and being congealed, settled like unto a yellow lump; but after pouring it out, the bellows blowing, there were found eight ounces and a little less than eleven grains of the purest gold.

A fatal blow?

Van Helmont was so impressed with this result that he christened his son Mercurius. Another 17th-century scientist, Rudolf Glauber, the German physician and chemist, believed that he had found one of the ingredients of the Philosopher's Stone in the waters of a spa where he had gone to take a cure. What he found was in fact sodium sulphate, which to this day we know as Glauber's salt – an effective laxative, but not capable of producing gold. No less a thinker than Sir Isaac Newton remained convinced of the possibility of transmutation; so did Descartes, the great French philosopher; and Leibniz, the great philosopher and mathematician. Even Robert Boyle, whose book, *The sceptical chymist*, is generally believed to have struck a fatal blow to any serious belief in alchemy, remained certain to the end of his days that transmutation was possible.

Why were all these scientists convinced that it was possible to change metals into gold? The concept is a very ancient one, which seems to answer to deep human motivations. It came to medieval Europe by way of the Arabs. When they invaded Egypt, which they called Khem, in the seventh century, the Arabs discovered that the

Below: a chemical laboratory of the 17th century, that of Rudolf Glauber. The furnace, A, contains a flask, B. Above the flask a 'pelican', D – a crude distillation device – delivers vapour into a series of vessels known as 'udels', F

Right: an Egyptian wall painting of 1300 BC shows goldsmiths (at the left of the two rows of figures), together with joiners. The smiths could make cheap alloys resembling gold and may have possessed the art of electroplating

Far left: Johann Friedrich Schweitzer, known frequently by the Latinised form of his name, Helvetius, was one of the many scientists who believed they had seen the production of gold from base metals

Egyptians were masters of the art of working in gold. They called gold-working *al-kimiya* – 'the art of the land of Khem' – and so, according to one account, the word 'alchemy' was born.

In the great library of Alexandria the Arabs discovered all the writings of the Greek philosophers – in particular those of Aristotle, who lived in the fourth century BC and who can truly be called the first great scientist. The Arabs had the manuscripts copied and translated into Arabic and they found their way all over the Arab world.

Aristotle believed that the material world was made from 'prime matter', which in itself lacked all physical properties, but on which different 'forms' could be impressed. Form was not merely physical shape, but every specific property of a body or a substance. Among these were four 'qualities': wetness, dryness, heat and cold. These qualities gave rise to four 'elements', or simple substances: fire, which was hot and dry; air (for example, steam) which was hot and wet; water, which was cold and wet; earth, which was cold and dry.

From this scheme of things it was very easy to progress to the idea that every substance was composed of all four elements in various proportions. For instance, consider a piece of green wood heated over a fire. First, water appears in droplets at the end of the wood; then steam and vapour are given off; then the wood burns, apparently releasing fire; and finally ash, or earth, is left. To change one substance into another, therefore, it was only necessary to change the proportions of elements in them by addition or subtraction.

Advances in alchemy

Faced with the impressive skills of the Egyptian metal workers, who knew how to colour cheaper metals to make them look like gold, the Arabs naturally supposed that their secret lay in the application of Aristotle's theories. For hundreds of years Arab scientists experimented in their laboratories. They made many important chemical discoveries and they invented most of the apparatus that is still used by chemists today. But they did not discover how to turn base metal into gold. However, one of the earliest Arab philosophers, Jabir ibn Hayyan, made an important contribution to the development of alchemical theory.

Aristotle had regarded the smoke produced in burning as earthy, and contrasted it with the watery vapour produced when water boils. Stones and minerals that were unchanged by the fire supposedly consisted mainly of this earthy smoke, while metals, which became liquid, were formed from the watery vapour.

Jabir suggested that the vapour produced by boiling water was an intermediate stage in its transformation into air. The vapour could be transformed into a material he called

Good as gold

Mankind recognised very early that gold, being virtually indestructible, non-rusting, yet highly malleable, was an ideal medium of exchange. The economy of the major powers is still based on it. Gold almost always appears in the metallic state, commonly in seams or nuggets. Alluvial gold is found deposited in the beds of rivers that have been carrying gold-bearing rocks away for millions of years. Pyrites, or 'fool's gold', is often found close by.

The assaying, or testing, of gold has always been a matter of high importance. Gold jewellery, which must not be damaged, can be weighed and its volume can be measured in order to determine its density: alloys are generally less dense than gold of high purity. In addition, the metal is 'touched' to a touchstone, such as a piece of black jasper, a variety of quartz. The colour of the mark made by gold is different from that made by gilt, brass or copper alloys.

Right: Aristotle's scheme of the four elements. Each possesses the two neighbouring 'qualities'. The earth, water, air and fire with which we are familiar are more or less impure approximations to these ideal substances

Below: the scientist Jan Baptista van Helmont added his voice in support of the reality of transmutation

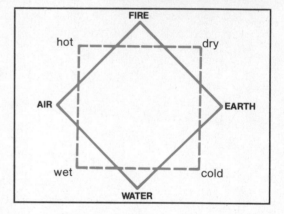

mercury, though this was not the familiar metal, but an ideal substance combining the qualities of lustre and liquidity. Earthy smoke was likewise earth in the process of becoming air, and it could be turned into 'sulphur', which combined the qualities of earthiness and combustibility. The various metals and minerals were formed in the earth from combinations of mercury and sulphur.

Jabir investigated what happened when he distilled a wide variety of organic materials – that is, substances derived from living things. In every case he obtained a liquid, which he identified as the element water since it was cold and wet; an 'oil', which, being hot and wet, must be air; a coloured substance – a tincture – that burned, which he thought to be the element fire; and a dry black residue, which he identified as the element earth. He had thus, he believed, isolated the four elements of Aristotle.

He then set out to purify these elements

If a piece of gold-bearing ore is to be assayed, the gold is first extracted. The ground ore is heated in a fireclay crucible with lead oxide and charcoal; molten lead settles at the bottom of the crucible as an alloy with any gold and silver present in the ore. The other mineral contents form a floating liquid slag.

The lead 'button' is then heated gently in a small 'cupel', a vessel made of bone ash. The lead turns back into lead oxide, which is absorbed into the cupel, leaving a bead of gold and silver – together, perhaps, with a small amount of platinum. The silver is 'parted' from the gold by being dissolved in hot dilute nitric acid.

Medieval alchemists discovered that gold would not dissolve in nitric, sulphuric or hydrochloric acids – but that it would dissolve in aqua regia, a mixture of nitric and hydrochloric acids. This led to serious misapprehension, since it was often assumed that anything that dissolved in aqua regia (and a great many substances will do so) was thus proved to be gold.

Right: how Jabir ibn Hayyan modified the theory of Aristotle. Like the original four elements, his 'mercury' and 'sulphur' are idealised substances. They combine, respectively, the qualities of lustre and liquidity, and earthiness and combustibility

Below: the Arab alchemist Jabir, in a fanciful European representation of the 17th century

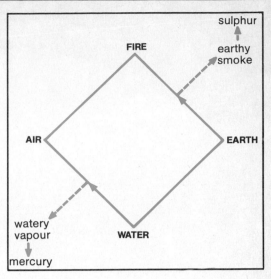

and isolate each *quality*. By distilling water 700 times, he wrote, he had obtained a brilliant white substance, which crystallised like salt. This, he said, was the purified quality of coldness. He supposed that he would be able to prepare pure moistness from his 'oil', pure dryness from his 'earth', and pure heat from his 'tincture'. He described the last as a transparent substance, brilliant, lustrous and red. This was the substance that the European alchemists named the Philosopher's Stone.

The philosophy of the Greeks returned to Europe, together with all the additions made by the Arabs, when Moslem rule was ended in Toledo, in central Spain, towards the end of the 11th century, and Christian scholars were able to translate the Arabic manuscripts in the library there. Soon after, many Europeans began to experiment with alchemy: they included Albrecht, a churchman and philosopher who became known as 'Albertus Magnus' and was renowned for the breadth and profundity of his learning; Roger Bacon, the learned doctor of Oxford University; and Philippus Aureolus Theophrastus Bombastus von Hohenheim.

This arrogant, boastful, colourful character has given his name to all the languages of Europe, for we now describe such a man as 'bombastic'. But he preferred to call himself Paracelsus, implying that he was greater than Celsus, the first-century writer who had been regarded as the greatest authority on medical matters. It was Paracelsus, writing in an extraordinary mixture of Latin, German and invented words, who took the Arabic word for black eye-paint, *al-kohl*, and gave it to

spirits of wine, which has borne the name 'alcohol' ever since. From the German *all-Geist* he made up the word 'alkahest', denoting a supposed universal solvent that would convert all bodies into their prime matter. And from Jabir's theory of elemental sulphur and mercury he developed an alchemical principle that seems to reveal some kind of intuitive understanding of 20th-century physics (see page 92). His influence was to be a crucial stimulus to the slow development of modern chemistry. But the pursuit of the Philosopher's Stone and the Elixir of Life was still very far from over.

Right: title page from the 1603 edition of the works of Paracelsus. The author himself is portrayed at the head of the page, and the figure on the right is a representation of Hermes Trismegistos, whose principle 'as above, so below' was the basis of all medieval magical experimentation

The Elixir of Life

One of the aims of the alchemist's work was the discovery of the Philosopher's Stone and the Elixir of Life. This chapter describes one alchemist who was rumoured to have succeeded

'ALWAYS DRUNK AND ALWAYS LUCID' was how a biographer described Theophrastus Bombastus von Hohenheim, who gave himself the name 'Paracelsus'. His career included the study of magic under Hans von Trittenheim at Würzburg in Germany, working for a year at the mining school of Sigismund Fugger, travelling through Germany, Italy, France, the Netherlands, England, Scandinavia and Russia, serving as an army surgeon in Italy and taking a medical degree at the University of Ferrara. He was appointed city physician of Basel, in Switzerland, in 1526, and he celebrated his appointment with a remarkable tirade in the city square.

In one hand he held a brass pan full of glowing coals. Into the fire he thrust the works of Avicenna, the 11th-century Arab philosopher, and of Galen, the second-century Greek medical authority. He sprinkled sulphur and saltpetre over them so that they were consumed in spectacular flames, and spoke:

If your physicians only knew that their prince Galen – they call none like him – was sticking in Hell, from whence he has sent letters to me, they would make

Above: alchemists grew old and decrepit in their quest for the Elixir of Life. Yet stories persist that some fortunate practitioners found some way to survive beyond their natural span

Below: Theophrastus Bombastus von Hohenheim, city physician of Basel, contributed much to alchemical theory, as well as to pharmacy

the sign of the cross upon themselves with a fox's tail. In the same way your Avicenna sits in the vestibule of the Infernal portal; and I have disputed with him about his . . . Tincture of the Philosophers, his Quintessence, and Philosopher's Stone . . . and all the rest. O you hypocrites, who despise the truths taught you by a great physician [he meant himself]. . . . Come then, and listen, impostors who prevail only by the authority of your high positions! After my death, my disciples will burst forth and drag you to the light, and shall expose your dirty drugs, wherewith up to this time you have compassed the death of princes. . . .

In spite of his overweening, egotistical style, Paracelsus was an important influence in the development of the science of pharmacy. He was among the first to recognise that the processes of alchemy were the same as those of baking and cooking – he even dignified the man who lit and tended the fires with the title of 'alchemist'. And he replaced the four elements of Aristotle (see page 82) by three 'hypostatical principles': mercury, sulphur and salt. The term 'hypostatical' meant that these were not the ordinary substances: they were, rather, three ideal substances, which a 17th-century text described in these terms:

Mercury is that sharp, permeating, ethereal and very pure fluid to which all nutrition, sense, motion, power, colours and retardation of age are due. It is derived from air and water; it is the food of life. . . .

Sulphur is that sweet, oleaginous and viscid [glutinous] balsam conserving the natural heat of the parts, instrument of all vegetation [unconscious activity of plants or animals, such as assimilating food], increase and transmutation, and the fountain and origin of all colours. It is inflammable, yet has great power of conglutinating [sticking together] extreme contraries.

Salt is that dry saline body preserving mixtures from putrefaction, having wonderful powers of dissolving, coagulating, cleansing, evacuating, conferring solidity, consistency, taste and the like. It resembles earth, not as being cold and dry, but as being firm and fixed.

Paracelsus saw these three principles in terms of spirit (mercury), soul (sulphur) and body (salt). As he himself put it in one of his alchemical writings:

But as there are many kinds of fruit, so there are many kinds of sulphur, salt and mercury. A different sulphur is in gold, another in silver, another in lead, another in iron, tin, etc. Also a different one in sapphire, another in the emerald, another in the ruby, chrysolite, amethyst, magnets, etc. Also

Two targets of the wrath of Paracelsus: the Greek writer Galen (above), an authority on drugs, and the Arab ibn Sina, known in Europe as Avicenna (below), author of *The canon of medicine*

another in stones, flint, salts, spring-waters, etc. . . .

This kind of thinking led Paracelsus to the search for the 'quintessence' of each material, the refined and purified extract that was the essential part of it. Supposedly he identified this with the 'mercury' specific to that substance. In his public speech in Basel he was contrasting the quintessences of various metals, which he had prepared by distillation, to common 'dirty drugs'.

An innovation in alchemy

The concept of hypostatic mercury, sulphur and salt gave a new impetus to alchemical enquiry; and Paracelsus achieved apparent success in medical treatment with some of his 'quintessences'. They were probably weak acid solutions, pepped up in some instances with alcohol.

The ideas of Paracelsus also encouraged the search for the Elixir of Life. This remarkable substance, which supposedly conferred longevity or even immortality, had reputedly been discovered already. It was important in Chinese alchemy, the story of which will be told later (see page 88). In Europe alchemists were rumoured at various times to have gained immortality. One was Nicolas Flamel.

Flamel was a thrifty and industrious scrivener (a scribe and copyist) in 14th-century Paris. In 1357 he bought a very old and large illuminated book:

The cover of it was of brass, well bound, all engraven with letters or strange figures. . . . This I know that I could not read them nor were they either Latin or French letters. . . . As to

What was the Philosopher's Stone?

Early philosophers were convinced that by lengthy processes of purification it must be possible to extract from minerals the natural 'principle' that supposedly caused gold to 'grow' in the earth. The anonymous 17th-century book *The sophic hydrolith* tells us that the Philosopher's Stone is prepared from a mineral by first 'purging it of all that is thick, nebulous, opaque and dark', yielding mercurial water or 'water of the Sun', which has a pleasant penetrating smell and is very volatile.

Part of this liquid is put on one side, and the rest mixed with one twelfth its weight of 'the divinely endowed body of gold' – ordinary gold being useless because it is defiled by daily use. The mixture forms a solid amalgam, which is then heated gently for a week. It is then dissolved in some of the mercurial water in an egg-shaped phial.

Then the remaining mercurial water

Gold had to be added to the Philosopher's Stone to make further gold. This is symbolised here by the lion devouring the serpent in order to transform it

is added gradually, in seven portions; the phial is sealed, and kept at such a temperature as will hatch an egg. After 40 days, the phial's contents will be as black as a raven's head; after seven more days small grainy bodies like fish-eyes appear.

The Philosopher's Stone begins to make its appearance: first reddish in colour; then white, green and yellow like a peacock's tail; then a dazzling white; and later a deep glowing red. Finally, 'the revivified body is quickened, perfected and glorified' and appears of a most beautiful purple colour.

Gradually, over the centuries, alchemists came to identify the Philosopher's Stone with the Elixir, the substance that would confer eternal life.

As for the mineral from which the Stone was to be prepared, *Gloria mundi* (1526) says it is 'familiar to all men, both young and old, is found in the country, in the village, in the town. . . . No-one prizes it, though, next to the human soul, it is the most beautiful and most precious thing upon earth. . . .'

For 21 years Flamel tried without success to find someone who could explain these pictures to him. At last his wife Perrenelle suggested that he should travel to Spain to seek out some learned Jew who could shed light on the matter. Flamel decided to make the famous pilgrimage to the shrine of St James at Compostela; and so, with his pilgrim's staff and broad-brimmed hat, and carrying carefully made copies of the mysterious illustrations, he set out on foot.

When he had made his devotions at the shrine, he travelled on to the city of León, in northern Spain, where by chance he made the acquaintance of a certain Master Canches, a learned Jewish physician. When he saw the pictures, he was 'ravished with great astonishment and joy', recognising them as parts of a book that he had long believed lost. He made up his mind at once to return with Flamel to France. But at Orléans, wearied and old, he died. Flamel, having seen him buried, returned alone to Paris.

I had now the *prima materia*, the first principles, yet not their first preparation, which is a thing most difficult, above all things in the world. . . . Finally, I found that which I desired, which I also knew by the strong scent and odour thereof. Having this, I easily accomplished the Mastery. . . . The first time that I made projection [accomplished transmutation] was upon Mercury, whereof I turned half a pound [227 grams], or thereabouts,

the matter that was written within, it was engraved (as I suppose) with an iron pencil or graver upon . . . bark leaves, and curiously coloured. . . .

On the first page was written in golden letters: 'Abraham the Jew, Priest, Prince, Levite, Astrologer and Philosopher, to the Nation of the Jews dispersed by the Wrath of God in France, wisheth Health'. Flamel subsequently referred to this manuscript as 'the book of Abraham the Jew'. The dedication was followed by execrations against anyone who was neither priest nor scribe and who might read the book. As Flamel was a scribe, he was emboldened to read further.

The author intended to give the dispersed Jews assistance in paying their taxes to the Roman authorities by teaching them how to transmute base metals into gold. The instructions were clear and easy to follow, but unfortunately they referred only to the later stages of the process. The only guidance to the earlier stages was said to be in the illustrations given on the fourth and fifth leaves of the book. To his great disappointment, Flamel found that, although these pictures were well painted,

yet by that could no man ever have been able to understand it without being well skilled in their Qabalah, which is a series of old traditions, and also to have been well studied in their books.

Left and above left: two pages from an early copy of 'The book of Abraham the Jew' in Paris. The lower picture shows those who seek for gold in the garden; the figure at bottom right, if we may believe Ninian Bres, is Nicolas Flamel himself. In the upper picture, titled 'the three colours of the work', the rider mounted on a black lion represents gold in maceration; the second, on a red lion, represents the inner ferment; and the crowned rider on a white lion symbolises success

Left: a supposed portrait of Nicolas Flamel, from an early 19th-century work

Right: another picture from 'The book of Abraham the Jew'. This has been called 'the fair flower on the mountain'. The red and white flowers stand for stages in the Great Work, the dragons for sophic (that is, 'ideal') mercury, and the griffins for a combination of the lion (the fixed principle) and the eagle (the volatile principle)

COMMENT LES INOCENS FVRENT OCCIS PAR LE COMMANDEMENT DV ROY HERODES
Nicolas Flamel.

Above: an 18th-century engraving of the frescoes that were painted for Flamel in the churchyard of the Holy Innocents in Paris, and which had survived for 400 years. A pair of small figures below the centre represent Flamel and his wife Perrenelle, while the panels at the top show seven of the illustrations from 'The book of Abraham the Jew'. Numerous copies of these pictures were made over the centuries, and it is now very difficult to determine what was in the original

into pure silver, better than that of the Mine, as I myself assayed, and made others assay many times. This was upon a Monday, the 17th of January about noon, in my home, Perrenelle only being present, in the year of the restoring of mankind 1382.

Three months later Flamel made his first transmutation into gold. He and Perrenelle put their new-found wealth to good use: they endowed

fourteen hospitals, three chapels and seven churches, in the city of Paris, all which we had new built from the ground, and enriched with great gifts and revenues, with many reparations in their churchyards. We also have done at Boulogne about as much as we have done at Paris, not to speak of the charitable acts which we both did to particular poor people, principally to widows and orphans. . . .

After Flamel's death in 1419 the rumours began. Hoping that the Philosopher's Stone might still be hidden in one of his houses, people searched through them again and again, until one was reduced to a pile of rubble. There were stories that both Perrenelle and Nicolas were still alive; that she had gone to live in Switzerland while he buried a log in her grave, and that later he did the same at his own 'funeral'.

In the centuries since, legends have persisted that the wealthy alchemist had defeated death. The 17th-century traveller Paul Lucas, while travelling in Asia Minor, met a distinguished Turkish philosopher. He was told that

true philosophers had had the secret of prolonging life for anything up to a thousand years. . . . At last I took the liberty of naming the celebrated Flamel, who, it was said, possessed the Philosopher's Stone, yet was certainly dead. He smiled at my simplicity, and asked with an air of mirth: Do you really believe this? No, no, my friend, Flamel is still living; neither he nor his wife has yet tasted death. It is not above three years since I left both . . . in India; he is one of my best friends.

A couple who cheated death

In 1761 Flamel and his wife were said to have attended the opera in Paris. Still later there were stories very reminiscent of those concerning the Count St Germain, who was also supposed to have discovered the secret of the Elixir of Life. What are we to make of that almost unknown work *Le corbeau menteur* (*The lying raven*) by the 19th-century writer Ninian Bres?

He was a little less than middle height, stooping somewhat with the weight of years, but still with a firm step and a clear eye, and with a complexion strangely smooth and transparent, like fine alabaster. Both he and the woman with him – clearly his wife, although she appeared almost imperceptibly the older and more decisive of the two – were dressed in a style that seemed only a few years out of fashion and yet had an indefinable air of antiquity about it. I stood, half-concealed in a little archway toward the end of the Boulevard du Temple: my hands were stained with acid, and my topcoat stank of the furnace. As the couple came abreast of the spot where I stood, Flamel turned toward me and seemed about to speak, but Perrenelle drew him quickly on, and they were almost at once lost in the crowd. You ask how I am so confident that this was Nicolas Flamel? I tell you that I have spent many hours in the Bibliothèque Nationale, poring over the book of Abraham the Jew. Look carefully at the first side of the fifth leaf and there, in the lower right-hand corner of the representation of those who seek for gold in the garden, you will see the face that searched mine that evening on the Boulevard du Temple, and that has haunted my dreams ever since. . . .

Alchemy in both East and West was concerned with the purification of the soul as much as with the transmutation of metals. This chapter relates the two traditions to each other and to primitive magic

ALCHEMY GATHERED into its literature a whole bestiary of symbols: the black crow; the white pelican, its breast spotted red with its own blood, on which, by popular belief, its young fed; the phoenix; the dove; the peacock, with its tail of wonderful colours; red and green lions; dragons of all hues. There were human symbols as well: the red man and the white woman, sometimes twined together in sexual union; the king murdered by his own son; and above all the androgyne, or hermaphrodite, which represented the combination of opposites that produced the Philosopher's Stone.

The symbols are so striking and so numerous that they caught the attention of the psychologist Carl Jung, who devoted a whole book to them. Throughout his life, Jung had studied the way in which the same kind of symbols appear to have the same kind of meaning in communities and cultures widely separated in time or place. It was, Jung thought, as if these symbols were a part of mankind's fundamental make-up.

One of Jung's predecessors was Herbert Silberer. In his book *Problems of mysticism and its symbolism* he attaches great importance to the work of one of the first alchemists to set his thoughts down in writing, Zosimos of Panopolis, in Egypt. Zosimos, who lived about AD 300, wrote down some of the secrets of alchemy in terms of a strange vision:

> I asked him who he was and in a feeble voice he answered me: I am he-who-is, the priest of the sanctuary, and I am overwhelmed by another's strength. For at break of day came a deputy who

Alchemy: sex and symbolism

Above: when lead is kept molten in a basin over a furnace, it will form an encrustation of bright yellow crystals of lead oxide, or litharge. Here the aged Saturn symbolises lead, while the gold-crested white dove is the 'sublime' spirit of the lead, its quintessence. That, at least, is one interpretation of this illustration from the 16th-century manuscript *Splendor solis*, but several other equally plausible explanations have been proposed

Right: in this woodcut from *The new pearl of great price* (1546), the crowned king is gold, killed by his son Mercury. After many vicissitudes he rises again

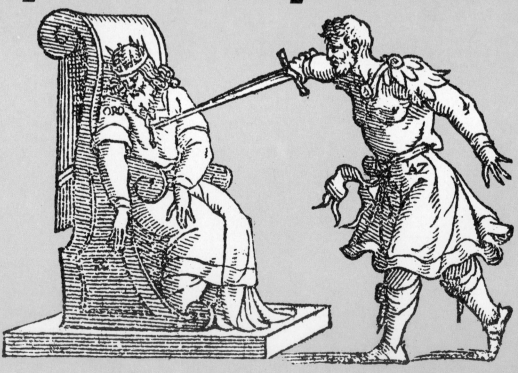

swiftly seized me, cleaving me with a sword and dividing me in pieces; and after flaying all the skin from my head he mixed my bones with my flesh and burned them in the fire. . . .

When we look at the illustrations from alchemical works written some 1200 years later, or read the descriptions of the Great Work, it is not really surprising to find the same kind of imagery employed, for in this instance it is easy to trace a direct line of descent. But what is remarkable is to compare the vision of Zosimos with the visions of the shamans, the priests of the nomadic tribes of Siberia and North America.

As adolescents, future shamans were suddenly seized by a 'sickness', a kind of divine madness that was the first sign of their priestly vocation. During this phase they saw extraordinary visions. One future shaman, for instance, described how he saw himself enter a mountain, where a naked man was working a bellows to keep a cauldron heating on a fire. The man seized the shaman with a great pair of tongs, cut off his head and sliced up his body, and threw everything into the cauldron, where it cooked for three years. There were three anvils in the cave, and on one of them the man forged the shaman's head; then he rescued the bones, joined them together, and covered them with flesh.

The mystique of the metalworker

Many of the initiation visions seen by the shamans took similar forms to this, and the famous anthropologist Mercia Eliade has shown that they are closely related to the high priestly standing enjoyed by metalworkers among primitive peoples.

In some very early mythologies, the Sun was seen as plunging every evening into the womb of Earth, sowing the 'seed' of the metals. It was supposed that the metals gradually developed, passing through various stages, until the final result was gold. (We have seen how even the scientist Aristotle believed that the Earth somehow 'bred' metals – see page 84.)

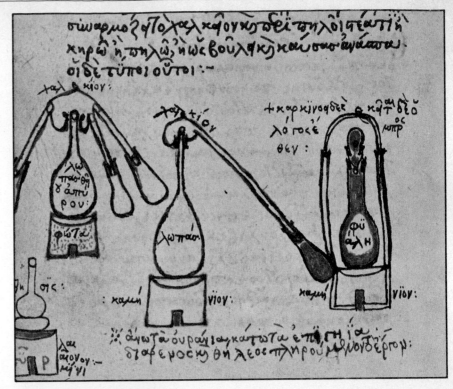

Top: a 15th-century copy of an alchemical treatise by Zosimos of Panopolis

Above: a travelling Tuareg silversmith from Niger. These artisans are often outcasts, regarded with fear and awe

Left: another tantalising illustration from *Splendor solis*. A fair white woman offers a scarlet cloak to a man emerging from primeval blackness into a ruddy form that is reminiscent in some ways of a new-born child

Metalworkers, who knew how to take mineral ores and, by smelting them in a womb-shaped furnace, to produce metals, and who further understood how to shape the metal produced, were thus performing much the same kind of marvel as the Sun-god himself. They were venerated as priests who stood closer than ordinary men to the god.

It was natural to suppose that, if a man could make himself truly god-like, he would gain the power to transform baser metals into gold, by exactly the same processes that they underwent in the Earth. This belief was expressed on the Emerald Tablet, a record said to have been inscribed by the god Thoth, who was supposed to have taught the ancient Egyptians the sciences and the art of writing. (The Greeks identified Thoth with one form of their god Hermes – Hermes Trismegistos, the 'thrice-great'. Hence the term 'hermetic art' for alchemy.)

The principle of the Emerald Tablet can be expressed in a phrase widely used by alchemists: 'as above, so below'. The tablet appears to have carried a set of mystical instructions for the manufacture of gold by transmutation – the 'operation of Sol'. The seventh of these precepts reads: 'Separate the earth from the fire, the subtle from the gross, acting prudently and with judgement.' The eighth reads: 'Ascend with the greatest sagacity from the Earth to heaven, and then again descend to the Earth, and unite together the powers of things superior and things inferior. . . .' These can be read as straightforward metaphors for separating and recombining elements. The 'ascent' and 'descent' could refer to the circulatory action of a kerotakis, a type of still.

But on another level these same precepts

alchemy of the Arabs (as it was later transmitted to medieval Europe) and that of the Far East, the Chinese alchemists were also concerned with the attainment of immortality. They were undoubtedly very interested in the production of gold, but principally for its value as an elixir. The substance with which they attempted to prolong life was cinnabar, a bright-red compound of two of the vital substances of western alchemy: mercury and sulphur.

The ancient philosophy of Tao is concerned with the delicate blending of two fundamental energies: *yin*, the feminine principle, and *yang*, the masculine. The careful commingling of *yin* and *yang* was believed to be a means of prolonging life.

At the lower levels of Taoist practice, the mixing of *yin* and *yang* could be achieved by controlled sexual intercourse; the more advanced mystics practised various meditative procedures, designed to bring about a kind of 'distillation' of *yang* within the body. These practices were commonly known as 'sexual alchemy'.

The body was seen as a tier of three crucibles (*tan-t'ien*) on a central column. The lowest, the cauldron or three-footed furnace, was in the belly below the solar plexus; the second was behind the solar plexus; the third between the eyes.

The 'prime substance' of this inner alchemy was the primitive sexual energy, *ching*, residing in the lowest crucible. It was one of three forces, the others being *ch'i*, the moving vitality, in the middle crucible and *shen*, the luminous personal spirit, in the upper crucible. Meditation began with rhythmical deep breathing: the 'heavenly fire of the heart' began to circulate and was impelled – as if by a bellows – down to the furnace in the belly. Gradually, as energy rose up the 'distillation column' of the spine, the content of *yang* increased; then, as it

could be, and were, taken as referring to a spiritual work of self-purification – a long and arduous liberation of the divine part of the alchemist's nature from the grossness of his body and senses.

All these various strands came together: the primitive belief that the search for a way to transmute base metals into gold involved a succession of god-like actions developed into the belief that an important part of alchemy was the attempt to become like God – 'as above, so below'. From this, no doubt, stems the conviction that the final result of the alchemical quest was to achieve eternal life.

It is striking that, although there is no evidence of any connection between the

Above: the Emerald Tablet, as it was imagined by Heinrich Khunrath in his *Amphitheatrum sapientiae aeternae* (*Amphitheatre of eternal wisdom*), which was first published in 1609. Below the Latin text, Khunrath provides a translation into German

An experiment with immortality

The Tao master Wei Po-Yang went into the mountains one day, accompanied by three disciples and his white dog. The master had concocted a certain 'gold medicine', reputed to be the Elixir of Immortality. He fed a little of the medicine to his dog, which promptly died. Wei Po-Yang said to his disciples: 'To live without taking the medicine would be just the same as to die of the medicine. I must take it.' He did so and, like the dog, expired.

Two of the grief-stricken disciples immediately set off to find implements with which to bury their late master. But the third, Yü by name, was more thoughtful; it seemed to him that Wei Po-Yang must have known what he was

doing. Yü therefore took some of the medicine himself, and also died.

A short while later, Wei Po-Yang revived, for his medicine had contained only enough impurity to cause temporary death. He put a little more of the medicine into the mouths of the dog and of Yü, both of whom also recovered after a few moments. Together, the three strolled off into immortality.

Wei Po-Yang lived in the second century AD, and he is credited with the authorship of the treatise *Ts'an-t'ung-ch'i* (*The three ways unified and harmonised*), a work that made Taoism into a coherent system. Among other things it deals with the 'pills of immortality', which, says Wei, are 'extremely efficacious, although their individual size is so small that they occupy only the point of a knife or the edge of a spatula.'

condensed at the top of the head and descended again, *yin* replaced *yang*. Eventually, the heat of the furnace was sufficient to drive the *ching*, transformed, up to the second crucible, where it combined with the *ch'i*. As in the alchemist's vessel known as a pelican, the two were continuously recycled, rising up the central column and then dropping back into the furnace for further purification. As the furnace was fanned to greater heat, the combined *ching* and *ch'i* eventually reached the *shen* in the upper crucible; and suddenly the 'inner copulation of the dragon and the tiger' took place. Su Tung P'o put it this way in AD 1110:

> The dragon is mercury. It is the semen and the blood. He issues from the kidneys and is stored in the liver. The tiger is lead. He is breath and bodily strength. He issues from the mind and the lungs bear him. When the mind is moved, breath and strength act with it. When the kidneys are flushed, then semen and blood flow. . . .

When the *ching-ch'i-shen* was rising and descending like liquid in a briskly bubbling still, it progressively purified until it was one with the energies of the cosmos. Then a special ambrosial fluid flowed like saliva in the mouth. Two lights, gold and silver, slowly descended into the furnace; the body's breathing ceased, to be replaced by the breathing of a foetus formed from the impregnation of the ambrosia by the gold and silver lights. Slowly, the foetus grew into a homunculus, a 'crystal child'; it rose slowly to the crown of the head, and was there born as an immortal.

The alchemy of Tantra

Taoist inner alchemy possesses a striking resemblance to the basic beliefs of Tantra, which is claimed to be the oldest religion of India. The Tantric meditator begins by visualising the inner central column of his spine, the *sushumna*, as the axis of the cosmos. Up the *sushumna* are strung a series of 'wheels', or *chakras*; there are usually six, with a seventh in the top of the skull. The lowest *chakra* is at the base of the pelvis, and here sleeps the serpent Kundalini, coiled around an inner phallus (*lingam*), with its tip in her mouth. By means of various yoga exercises Kundalini is awakened, straightens herself, and enters the bottom of the *sushumna*. The ultimate intention is that Kundalini shall ascend permanently to the top of the skull, where a transcendental sexual union takes place.

The postures that awaken Kundalini are frequently sexual, and even the Tantric ascetic will imagine an ideal girl as Kundalini ascends. The Tantric obtains his energy through sexual intercourse, and the woman is regarded as the possessor of particularly important power.

The Tantric yogi is credited with many abilities, of which one is the transmutation of

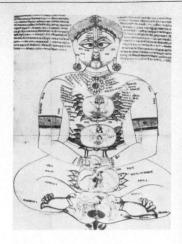

Above: in this Indian drawing from the 18th century, the 'subtle body' is represented as a plant growing from the ground. The *chakras*, or centres of energy positioned along the spinal *sushumna*, are shown symbolically by human and animal figures

Above and top right: the close symbolic relationship between Western alchemy and Tantric 'sexual alchemy' is clearly shown in these two pictures, one an Indian popular print of the early 19th century, the other a 16th-century European woodcut. In the upper illustration, the goddess Kali has beheaded herself, and her blood sprays onto the tongues of her attendants, while a couple make love in a lotus flower at her feet. The lower illustration shows the hermetic androgyne, a being formed when the son of Hermes and Aphrodite became united with the nymph Salmacis – a symbol of the union of opposites in chemical reactions

base metals into gold; even his urine and faeces may bring about transmutation. He recognises the importance of mercury and sulphur. As an ancient treatise puts it:

> When quicksilver is killed with an equal weight of sulphur it cures leprosy; when killed with thrice its weight of sulphur it cures mental languor; when it is killed with four times its weight of sulphur it removes grey hair and wrinkles; when it is killed by five times its weight of sulphur it cures consumption; when it is killed with six times its weight of sulphur it becomes a panacea for all the ills. . . .

The close similarity of the imagery – and the substances used – in alchemy in all these very different cultures is striking. A major difference is equally striking: that medieval European alchemy does not seem to have had any explicit sexual basis. It was not until ancient Taoist and Tantric manuscripts became available in translation toward the end of the 19th century that sex entered western alchemy. The magical society called the Golden Dawn taught some kind of esoteric link between the two; Karl Kellner, who founded the Ordo Templi Orientis (OTO) in 1906 was more explicit. And Aleister Crowley, who was a member of both secret societies, seized upon the connection with enthusiasm, and developed his own brand of sexual magic. And then the psychologists who found the symbolism of alchemy so fascinating were to teach that sex is at the heart of all human action.

Alchemy's hidden truth

In the 20th century science has achieved the alchemical dream of transmuting the elements. But modern alchemists still use traditional methods in pursuit of their quest.

THE GROWTH OF experimental science during the 18th and 19th centuries; the work of chemists such as Lavoisier, Priestley and Davy; the establishment of Dalton's atomic theory; and the subsequent discoveries of a host of scientists in all aspects of chemistry and physics – such developments should have sounded the death knell of alchemy. And yet they did not.

During the 19th and early 20th centuries, it is true, alchemists retreated into the mystical, spiritual aspects of their study. They were drawn into the Rosicrucianist occultism of societies such as the Golden Dawn and the Ordo Templi Orientis (OTO), which contrived to combine ill-digested snippets of oriental philosophy with the western European magical tradition.

Then, in 1919, the British physicist Ernest Rutherford announced that he had successfully achieved the transmutation of one element into another.

He had, in fact, changed nitrogen into oxygen. Admittedly, the amount of oxygen produced, some 20 parts per million, was minute, and the technique used, involving high-energy radiation, did not resemble in the slightest the procedures of the alchemists. But the experiment refuted the insistence of most scientists that transmutation was impossible, and all aspiring alchemists took heart.

It was in fact already known that transmutation took place in nature. The radioactive elements gradually 'decay', giving off radiation and producing further radioactive 'daughter' elements, which in turn decay. After a series of decays the end product, lead, is formed.

What Rutherford had done was to reverse the process. He had bombarded nitrogen gas with radiation consisting of fast-moving nuclei from the gas helium and had produced oxygen and hydrogen. The experiment can be expressed very simply in terms of atomic numbers (the chemical properties of each element are determined by its atomic number, which is the number of protons in its nucleus):

$$N(7) + He(2) = O(8) + H(1)$$

What every alchemist now asked himself was whether a similar kind of sum could be used

Opposite, top: the directors of the *Société Alchimique et Astrologique de France* in their laboratory in 1903. Despite the discoveries of 19th-century chemistry and physics, alchemy refused to die. The magazine that featured this picture said: 'To turn astrology into a true science, in which there is no room for fantasy – this is what they preach in their journal, *Rosa Alchemica'*

Opposite, below: the young Adolf Hitler (far left), with his patron, Erich Ludendorff. In association with Franz Tausend (centre), Ludendorff formed Company 164 to 'manufacture' gold. As a result they were able to divert 400,000 marks into Nazi Party funds. Tausend set up his gold-production laboratory at a quarry near Munich (right)

as a guide to the conversion of lead (82) into gold (79). Or perhaps another element might be a better starting point?

One of those who took renewed inspiration from the results of this experiment was a 36-year-old chemical worker in Munich, Franz Tausend. He had a theory about the structure of the elements that was a peculiar blend of the beliefs of Pythagoras, who had regarded the Universe as a combination of musical harmonies, and the discoveries of modern chemistry.

Tausend had published a pamphlet called *180 elements, their atomic weight, and their incorporation in a system of harmonic periods.* He believed that every atom had a frequency of vibration characteristic of that element, related to the weight of the atom's nucleus and to the grouping of electrons in orbital rings around it. Later research showed that this part, at least, of his theory was basically true. Tausend went on, however, to suggest that matter could be 'orchestrated': by adding the right substance to an element, it should be possible to change its vibration frequency into that of another element.

In 1924 Adolf Hitler was sent to prison for attempting to organise an armed uprising; one of his fellow conspirators, General Erich Ludendorff, was acquitted and in the following year stood for election as President of the German Republic. After being resoundingly defeated by the national hero Hindenburg, he turned his attention to raising funds for the infant Nazi Party. There were rumours

in government circles that a certain Tausend had succeeded in making gold by transmutation, and Ludendorff got together a group of industrialists and businessmen to investigate the matter.

On Tausend's instructions one of the group, the merchant Stremmel, purchased the necessary materials – mainly iron oxide and quartz. They were melted together in a crucible, which Stremmel then took to his hotel bedroom for the night so that it could not be tampered with. In the morning, Tausend heated the crucible again in his electric furnace, in the presence of his visitors, and then added a small quantity of white powder to the molten mass. When the crucible had cooled it was broken open, and a gold nugget weighing a quarter of an ounce (7 grams) was found inside.

Financing the Nazis

Ludendorff was overjoyed and immediately set about forming a company, which he called 'Company 164' – a number that, intriguingly, is twice the atomic number of lead. Ludendorff was to receive 75 per cent of the profits and Tausend 5 per cent. Investment money poured in and within a year the General had managed to divert some 400,000 marks into Nazi Party funds. Then, in December 1926, he resigned, leaving Tausend to handle all the debts. Nevertheless, Tausend contrived to continue raising money and on 16 June 1928 allegedly made 25 ounces (723 grams) of gold in a single

---

Atomic alchemy

Rutherford's work strengthened the conviction of orthodox scientists that the methods of the alchemists could never lead to the transmutation of elements. It was found that the atom has a central nucleus consisting of particles called protons, with positive electrical charge, and an equal or greater number of neutrons, lacking charge. Relatively light negatively charged electrons orbit the nucleus and fix the atom's chemical properties. The number of electrons is equal to the number of protons in the nucleus, so that the atom's positive and negative electrical charges balance.

So to change one element into another it is necessary to change the number of protons in the nucleus of each atom. The nucleus must be bombarded with fast-moving particles – either to force in additional protons or to disrupt the atom so that it loses protons. Today physicists use particles artificially accelerated by 'atom-smashing' machines. And they insist that chemical processes affect only the outer electrons, not the atom's deep interior.

Above: a modern particle-accelerating device

Left: Rutherford bombarded nitrogen atoms (seven protons, seven neutrons) with alpha particles (two protons bound to two neutrons), forming fluorine atoms (nine protons, nine neutrons). These lost a proton, forming a type of oxygen (eight protons, nine neutrons)

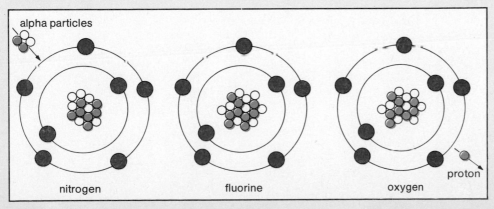

alpha particles

nitrogen   fluorine   oxygen   proton

operation. On the strength of this he was able to issue a series of share certificates, each to the value of 22 pounds (10 kilograms) of gold.

But when, a year or so later, no more gold had been produced, Tausend was arrested for fraud; and on 5 February 1931, after a sensational trial, he was found guilty and sentenced to four years' imprisonment. While awaiting trial he had succeeded in producing gold under strict supervision in the Munich Mint – but the evidence was contested in court and did not save him.

The same fate was to befall a Polish engineer named Dunikovski who, in the same year that Tausend was convicted, announced in Paris that he had discovered a new kind of radiation – 'z-rays' – which would transmute quartz into gold. The mineral, spread on copper plates, was melted by an electric discharge at 110,000 volts, and was then irradiated with the z-rays.

The world was becoming accustomed to new types of radiation with remarkable properties. x-rays had been discovered a few decades before. Three kinds of radiation – alpha, beta and gamma – had been identified in the emissions from radioactive substances. Intense 'cosmic' radiations had been discovered bombarding the Earth from space.

Rays with miraculous properties were a staple of futuristic fiction. The public was ready to believe that gold-creating rays could exist – even if their nature was rather inadequately explained by Dunikovski. Investors poured some two million francs into his process.

But within a few months, when no gold was forthcoming, he also was tried and found guilty of fraud. After two years in prison his lawyer succeeded in obtaining his release, and Dunikovski went with his family to San Remo in Italy, where he resumed his experiments.

Soon there were rumours that he was supporting himself by the occasional sale of lumps of gold. His lawyer, accompanied by the eminent chemist Albert Bonn, set out for San Remo to see for himself.

It was found that the quartz being used by Dunikovski already contained minute amounts of gold; but whereas the usual methods of extraction produced gold in quantities of only 10 parts per million, Dunikovski's methods yielded almost one hundred times as much. Each experiment, however, involved only minute quantities of quartz, so the quantity of gold produced was very small.

In October 1936 Dunikovski demonstrated his process before an invited group of scientists. He was very secretive about his apparatus, but gave a theoretical explanation that is reminiscent of the primitive origins of alchemy. He proposed that all minerals contained 'embryonic atoms' undergoing a transformation that in nature took many thousands of years to complete. He claimed that his process merely accelerated the natural growth of embryonic gold in quartz.

Making gold from sand

The demonstration attracted considerable attention and an Anglo-French syndicate was formed, which was to bring sand from Africa and treat it in a big new laboratory on the south coast of England. But the Second World War broke out and little more was heard of Dunikovski. There were rumours that he had established a factory on the Swiss-French border, and there were stories that when the Germans occupied France they manufactured gold to bolster their failing economy – but there is no proof.

There have been, and still are, many more practitioners of alchemy in the 20th century. One was Archibald Cockren, who was killed when a bomb struck his tiny laboratory during the blitz on London. He was a respected osteopath who practised gold therapy. He began his investigations with the metal antimony, then turned his attention to iron, copper, silver, mercury and gold. Then:

> I entered upon a new course of experiment, with a metal . . .with which I had had no previous experience. This metal, after being reduced to its salts

Above: an engraving from the 17th-century alchemical work *Atalanta fugiens*, illustrating the ubiquitous nature of the Philosopher's Stone. It may be of significance that the form of the Stone shown here could represent crystals of salt or sand

Left: the Polish engineer Dunikovski, escorted by police officers, leaves the Paris polytechnic where he had been demonstrating his alchemical process while awaiting trial for fraud

Above right: wringing out canvas sheets that have been spread to collect the morning dew. This illustration is from the alchemical treatise called *Mutus liber*

Right: Armand Barbault followed the directions of *Mutus liber* in his 20th-century alchemical work

and undergoing special preparation and distillation, delivered up the Mercury of the Philosophers, the Aqua Benedicta, the Aqua Coelestis, the Water of Paradise. The first intimation I had of this triumph was a violent hissing, jets of vapour pouring from the retort and into the receiver, like sharp bursts from a machine gun, and then a violent explosion, whilst a very potent and subtle odour filled the laboratory and its surroundings. . . .

Whatever Cockren's true achievement, nearly all his discoveries were lost in the bomb blast that killed him. A liquid that he called 'oil of gold' was used in later years, however, for medical purposes.

Postwar alchemy

Since the Second World War, much of the publicly known activity in alchemy has been centred in France. Apart from Eugène Canseliet, who claimed to have been a pupil of the mysterious Fulcanelli, and who has been seen on television at work in his laboratory, there were others such as the writer Roger Caro and the painter Louis Cattiaux.

But undoubtedly the most notorious was Armand Barbault. An essential part of the Barbault process was the gathering of dew in canvas sheets every morning between 21 March and 24 June. This is not a new idea: it is shown in the wordless book of engravings known as the *Mutus liber* ('silent book'), and it is recommended by Salmon in his *Polygraphica*: 'If you are indeed an Artist, you may by this turn all metals into their first matter.' Barbault described his first matter as a 'germ', which grew in black earth.

It is time to ask whether there might be any truth in the tales of the alchemists. Did competent scientists such as van Helmont, Schweitzer and Boyle really witness the transmutation of a base metal into gold? Did Archibald Cockren isolate the ideal 'mercury' and 'sulphur' sought by the alchemists? And did Tausend and Dunikovski really succeed

in producing gold from quartz?

Although the ancient alchemists could not possibly have had access to sources of energy sufficient to perform Rutherford's transmutation, perhaps they had some kind of intuitive understanding of what could happen. We wrote Rutherford's experiment as:

$$N(7) + He(2) = O(8) + H(1)$$

Now look at the three alchemical essentials postulated by Paracelsus: sulphur (symbol S, atomic number 16), mercury (symbol Hg, atomic number 80) and salt (sodium chloride, symbol NaCl – the atomic numbers of sodium and chlorine are 11 and 17, respectively). We can write a hypothetical reaction among these three as follows:

$$NaCl(28) + S(16) = NaS(27) + Cl(17)$$
$$NaS(27) + Hg(80) = Au(79) + NaCl(28)$$

Salt and sulphur are added together; chlorine gas is given off (to the alchemists this would simply have been 'air'); when mercury is added, the result is the original salt – and gold (Au).

The atomic numbers balance impressively. However, this is not the sort of reaction that ordinarily takes place in the chemical laboratory, where everything is either solid, liquid or gaseous. But there is a fourth state of matter, called plasma, in which atoms lose or gain electrons and can take part in chemical reactions that are impossible for them in their normal state. One of the easiest ways to produce a stream of plasma is to burn salt in the flame of the mundane Bunsen burner. Could this give a hint as to how the alchemists might have succeeded in bringing about 'impossible' reactions?

In our present state of knowledge, these are mere games with numbers. But they may bear further examination. Cockren began his research with antimony (Sb), but achieved his successes with 'a metal . . . with which I had had no previous experience.' He might have been referring to silicon (Si), which is not, in fact, a metal but a metalloid, belonging in a group of elements comprising carbon, germanium, tin and lead. It is the essential component of quartz, which is an almost pure compound of silicon and oxygen, silicon dioxide. We can easily write another 'Rutherford equation':

$$Si(14) + Si(14) + Sb(51) = Au(79)$$

A chance relationship among these atomic numbers? Or a guide to a possible gold-producing process involving silicon and antimony?

It seems improbable, despite the testimony that has accumulated over the centuries, that physical transmutation of a base metal into gold was ever achieved by any alchemist. But did those alchemists, striving to make themselves one with God, perhaps gain some intuitive understanding of the structure of matter? And when they described the Philosopher's Stone as 'the vilest and meanest of things . . . cast away and rejected by all', were they speaking of silicon dioxide – known to us as ordinary sand?

Index